HEALING THE ORIGINAL WOUND

Healing the Original Wound

Reflections on the Full Meaning of Salvation

Benedict Groeschel, C.F.R.

CHARIS

Servant Publications
Ann Arbor, Michigan

The Scripture quotations contained herein are from *The Revised Standard Version Bible, Catholic Edition,* copyright 1965 and 1966, by the Division of Christian Education of the National Council of the Churches of Christ in the USA, and are used by permission.

Published by Servant Publications
P.O. Box 8617
Ann Arbor, Michigan 48107

Cover design by Multnomah Graphics/Printing

96 97 10 9 8 7 6

Printed in the United States of America

ISBN 0-89283-778-0

Library of Congress Cataloging-in-Publication Data

Groeschel, Benedict J.
    Healing the original wound : reflections on the full meaning of salvation / Benedict Groeschel.
        p. cm.
    Includes bibliographical references.
    ISBN 0-89283-778-0
    1. Salvation 2. Spiritual life—Catholic Church. 3. Catholic Church—Doctrines. I. Title.
    BT751.2.G73 1993
    234—dc20   93-15174

Dedication

This book is gratefully dedicated to all who have read or listened to my work over the years and who have prayed for me to be able to be attentive to the Holy Spirit and to our one Teacher, Jesus Christ.

Contents

Preface / 9
Introduction / 11

1. The Original Wound / 15
2. Hope in the Midst of Hell: Our Justification / 43
3. Help My Unbelief / 69
4. Conversion: Our Struggle against the World / 101
5. Sheep among the Wolves / 131
6. Growing in Holiness / 163
7. The Door to Eternity / 189
8. The Last Things / 209

Epilogue: The Great Healing / 227
Notes / 231

Preface

EVERY YEAR FOR ALMOST TWO DECADES I have given an annual series of conferences in various churches in the New York City area. As director of the Office of Spiritual Development of the New York Archdiocese, I might be said to be, in some far-fetched way, responsible for the spiritual lives of all New Yorkers. Such a burden could easily lead a person to despair. I hope these conferences will offer tangible proof on Judgment Day that I tried to do something.

These days of recollection are aimed at sincere Christians seeking to deepen their spiritual lives and to open their hearts to others around them: families, friends, members of their religious community or parish, those with whom they work, and especially the poor and needy. Many of these conferences are eventually published on audio and then as videocassettes to be aired on Eternal Word Television Network. One series appeared as a book, *Stumbling Blocks and Stepping Stones*, published by Paulist Press. So far none has come to the final bounce as a Broadway musical.

When the editors of Servant Publications contacted me about making the 1989-90 series entitled "The Truths of Salvation" into a book, I explained that I was too busy with too many other manuscripts already in the works. They happily suggested that I work with Pam Moran who had experience helping others turn recorded material into books. Pam was a great help and made this volume possible.

In working through the final manuscript, I have added a number of insights and experiences which were not included in the original series—especially incidents from the lives of people touched by God whom I have met along the way in my work as a priest. I have obtained permission from all of these individuals, or their families in the case of deceased persons who had not given permission beforehand to use their stories anonymously.

You see, I don't really write any of my books. I have a profound conviction that I am simply an instrument—I hope—of the Holy Spirit. I feel he leads me to those who struggle toward salvation, and that I should then make their stories known to help others on the way. Meeting people who have responded to God's grace and trying to be a little help to them is what my life is all about—including anything that I write. I have no other interest, nor do my books have any other significance.

In writing this particular book concerning the truths of salvation, I have relied heavily on traditional theology, as well as contemporary applications made by Pope John Paul II, Hans von Balthasar, Karl Rahner, and Romano Guardini—even though I do not directly quote them.

I found the works of Peter Kreeft of Boston College, especially his *Fundamentals of the Faith,* so helpful that I advise all to read his books and in particular the excellent work of apologetics just cited. Professor Kreeft is one of a number of new apologists (mostly converts, by the way), who I hope will take the place of such heroes of my youth as G.K. Chesterton, Father Vincent McNabb, O.P., Frank Sheed, and Maisie Ward.

As always, I have relied very heavily on Scripture and on the writings of St. Augustine who has been my teacher for many years. I hope that you will find this book helpful and will pass it on to someone else. Let us pray for each other.

Benedict J. Groeschel, C.F.R.
St. Crispin Friary
Bronx, New York
Feast of Sts. Peter and Paul, 1992

Introduction

THERE IS REALLY ONLY ONE QUESTION of absolute significance in life and that is, are we going to be saved? All other questions, goals, and considerations, even those of love and justice, are absolutely related to this question. St. Augustine wrote long ago, "O rich man, do you have everything but you do not have God, you are nothing. O poor man, do you have nothing but you have God, you have everything." Salvation, the destiny of everlasting life and happiness in that mysterious reality we so pitifully and blandly call "heaven," is the bottom line. This book is about the ultimate meaning of life and death. If you are moved by the grace of God to recognize the importance of this mystery, or if you are healthy enough to care about your own future and that of those dear to you, then you ought to read this book. If you are not very interested in your ultimate fate as an individual right now, do not read this book. It will only upset you.

God has made us in his own image. The Creator of all has breathed life into us, including a unique capacity for sharing in his divine life for all eternity. The Catholic Church has been a profound instrument in the hands of God for imparting his love to his people and bringing the hope of life forever with him. Through the sacraments, through the priesthood and religious life, through the family, through the saints down through the ages, through ordinary people like you and me, God has showered grace upon grace on the human race. Sometimes it comes in buckets. Sometimes in torrents. Yet often we feel only the thinnest trickle. Many times we suffer through a severe drought.

We all hunger to know more about God and our own possible salvation. We want to draw closer to God himself. In this book, I would like to share with you some of my personal experiences and insights regarding the astonishing truths of our salvation. God is very mysterious, but we know that his mercies are indeed new every morning. Yet life is at times painful and bitter for us all. A friend of mine who has been a monk for many years sums it up in this way:

God is mysterious.
Adam and Eve messed life up.
Jesus called Judas "friend"
and Peter "Satan."
Jesus was crucified.
And you thought this was going to be a picnic.

This monk is a believer. He is a very serious Christian. He looks forward to eternity—but he is also a realist. He has been extremely ill for many years. He and I occasionally talk about the human condition and our one only really lasting hope. This book is an exploration of that hope and how it can be lived in our pagan society.

If you have loved and been loved in return, you have some idea of what the promise of eternal life is. You can think a little of the love of God. If you feel that you have been unloved or have not really loved, then you have a great hunger inside of you for the mysterious love of God. In either case, you know something about the imperative need, the restlessness, the hunger that we all have to find love, unfailing love, in the brief reality that we call our lives.

I hope a clearer picture of that hunger and of our desperate human condition will emerge in the pages that follow. Chapter one paints a graphic portrait of the devastation of sin, how it can absolutely gut the inside of a person and leave the poor soul for dead. Then we move on in search of some glimmer of light, some ray of hope in the midst of our own personal hell. Has God come to save us or not? Chapter two presents some stories of deliverance, how God calls us from death to life.

In chapter three, we examine the figure of Jesus Christ. Who is this Savior of the world? How has the supernatural changed our lives forever? Where can we expect to find him? Even if we believe, we all struggle to keep our heads above water at times. Chapter four addresses the modern tide of unbelief and how we can keep from getting sucked into its undercurrent. The daily struggles of life can leave us battered and exhausted. How can our Catholic faith be translated into victory, one day at a time?

Our personal walk with God is constantly interwoven with that of our brothers and sisters in Christ. Even though the Catholic Church has been brutally battered through the ages, and now is severely attacked in the media, how do we view the Catholic Church today? What place should it assume in each of our lives? How is God calling us to stand more firmly together in the face of media persecution? I address these issues in chapter five.

God calls each of us to be perfect, to be holy. I find that incredible! How can he restore the divine image in each of us? Chapter six looks at this seemingly impossible task. We often look at the saints as totally out in spiritual orbit, some place we can't go because we don't own a rocket ship. I don't know about you, but my soul's journey toward God usually proceeds at a snail's pace rather than leaping from one degree of glory to the next. Unfortunately, we usually lose patience with ourselves long before God does.

In chapter seven, we take a closer look at death and how people tend to think about what happens after life on the earth. How can we conquer our fear of death? Can we catch some glimpse of where God is taking us in the end? How can we make more sense of heaven and purgatory?

Finally, chapter eight discusses these questions in the light of God's firm intention to balance the scales of justice. How can we think about hell and the Final Judgment? And how do they jibe with the mercy of God, especially as personified in his only Son, Jesus Christ?

The Catholic Christian faith offers so many rich insights. Are you hungry to dwell on the truths of our salvation, food for the soul? Let us go into the fields ripe for the harvest.

ONE

The Original Wound

As a hart longs
for flowing streams,
so longs my soul
for thee, O God.
My soul thirsts for God,
for the living God.
When shall I come and behold
the face of God?
My tears have been my food
day and night,
while men say to me continually,
"Where is your God?" Ps 42:1-3

M Y FIRST MEMORY OF BETTY as a smiling little girl floated through my mind. As the years sped by she grew into a fine young woman—even in the midst of the violent and confusing world of East Harlem. Betty married a responsible young man. Despite the odds, together they began raising healthy children.

Then I pictured her only a few years later... praying fervently and desperately as we knelt before the casket of her husband. He had been shot to death right before Betty's eyes by a hit man who had the wrong address. I remembered her courage as she valiantly struggled in a flood tide of pain.

I reminisced about her second husband and their new family, with the five children waiting for me to unload the donated Christmas presents. I thought of the tiny fifth floor apartment—threadbare but sweetly decorated with proudly displayed school projects. I could still picture the black and white television that I had found for them, and the Cabbage Patch doll that Betty's daughter had so merrily received from one of our volunteers.

In place of these happy memories, I now clutched the five pathetic notes that Betty had penciled on little lined pieces of paper for her children, telling them that she loved them and would pray for them when she went home to God. Betty was dying of AIDS, contracted from her second husband—a drug user infected by an unsterilized needle.

As I descended on the elevator of Mount Sinai Hospital, I realized that I was angry... at God. Betty had never possessed much of this world's goods. She hadn't left Harlem more than a dozen times in her brief thirty-six years on earth. This Puerto Rican woman had only given of herself with that simple, powerful, instinctive love of a mother, without reserve and asking for nothing in return.

Unlike so many of her friends, Betty had come from an intact family of at least three generations. I had known them since they had come to New York City from San Juan, Puerto Rico. And three days after that visit to the hospital, I would be standing before the whole sorrowful clan to offer Betty's funeral Mass in the old church. How could I begin to wrap my mind and heart around such pain and desolation?

As I prepared to offer the funeral liturgy for this gentle soul now delivered from a miserable life, I suddenly realized I had been too angry to pray and really speak to God. Deep sorrow and frustration washed over me. The sight of her children and family crying in the front pews only heightened my conflicting emotions. I had tried to love God all my life... but I could not deny my anger and hurt.

Why? Why? Why! A question I had often asked in the face of senseless devastation.

As I began the Mass, the sunlight slanted through a huge stained glass window of the crucifixion of Jesus Christ. I stared at it during the Scripture readings. Without words or even deliberate thoughts, I realized how Christ had himself suffered the terrible effects of sin. Betty had been a victim of sin; so was her first husband who had been murdered; so was her second husband who shared in the desperation of so many trapped in the slums. Born into a hellhole where there are so few ways out, he had taken the easiest way—drugs. Now he was dying too.

I kept looking at the scene of the crucifixion, presented as it often is, as a gigantic theatrical tableau. Calvary was not like that at all. No doubt it was horrible, ugly, abhorrent, with only the nobility of Christ's prayer to relieve the degradation of it all.

I found no consolation in the scene, but at least I had some company in my confusion and question. *Why? Why have you forsaken me?* As Christ's soulful cry from the cross echoed in my mind, I fervently prayed that the Precious Blood of Jesus Christ would come down on all of us: on Betty's children and parents and family; on her husband in jail; on East Harlem; on our whole human scene of suffering and sorrow, including me.

The concluding prayers of the funeral liturgy remind us of the hope of salvation. When I lifted my eyes again, the sun had shifted so that the first dim rays of sunlight were coming through another window. Their tinted panes artistically rendered the resurrection, another greater-than-life theatrical tableau, another well-intentioned artist's failure to picture the unimaginable—a dead man coming back to life, a dead God rising in this miserable world. My spirit started to come back to life. I felt a deep stirring—not of joy, but of hope. These words of final farewell took on a very special meaning for me that day as I gave the funeral blessing over Betty's casket:

May the Angels lead you into Paradise.
May the Martyrs come to welcome you on your way,
And bring you to the Holy City, the New Jerusalem.
May the choir of Angels welcome you.

And with Lazarus who was once so poor,
May you have life everlasting—Betty.

With this hope firmly fixed in our minds, we start out on the journey through the pages of this book: a journey from sin to salvation, from wrath to peace, from death to life.

THE COSMIC DIMENSION

What is the cause of all these miseries? *Sin*. When the effects of sin explode in the human soul, the remains can look like an empty shell. A person may walk and talk, yet be spiritually and emotionally dead inside.

When we multiply the damage by the many billions of people who have inhabited this planet, what are the cosmic dimensions of such devastation? Natural disasters provide visible and audible evidence of a world "groaning in travail" as it eagerly awaits the revealing of the sons and daughters of God (Rom 8:22). As another graphic image of our desperate plight, few spectacles on earth can match the seething fury of a volcanic eruption.

While working on the conference that formed the basis of this book, I spent a week on Puget Sound in Seattle. Eager to do a little sightseeing, I got up at four one Sunday morning and drove south to see Mount St. Helens—a sight I imagined would display the power and majesty of God. Little did I know.

On the way, the beauty of the Douglas firs towering two hundred feet above me almost took my breath away. Nearer the mountain, I noticed warning signs marking the official escape route in case of volcanic activity—stark reminders that Mount St. Helens remains capable of a deadly eruption. Then I suddenly came upon a scene that you could never appreciate from a picture: one of utter devastation.

Mount St. Helens once rose majestically on the horizon, jutting into the sky in perfect symmetry, much like Japan's

Fujiyama. The white blanket of snow covering the cone-shaped peak had given little evidence of the molten rock beneath the surface of the earth. What was left after it erupted looks much like a ruined city, something like Hiroshima after World War II.

In 1980, thirteen hundred feet of the summit were blasted away—one-quarter of a cubic mile! The explosion had the cumulative effect of *five hundred atomic bombs*. The charred ground covered *five hundred square miles*. Fifty miles away, massive steel bridges over the interstate highway were swept downstream by a current of melting ice which carried along tons of ash and thousands of trees. These gruesome sights seem to hint at a different side to God's power and majesty.

I drove for about twenty minutes on a smooth new highway, with not one other car in sight. The ground was covered with several feet of ash. Denuded of branches and bark and charred to a black crisp, millions of trees spread out in perfect geometric order—like the spokes of a great wheel whose center was the crater of the volcano. The gaping hole itself was a gigantic wound in the earth, for which there is no cosmetic cure.

I stopped at a little store and talked to the clerk. "Were you here when the mountain erupted?" She answered, "Yes, it was terrible. We had to get snow plows to clean up the ash and it was dark for several days." I asked, "How far is it?" "Well, just a couple of miles down the road you'll get into the volcanic area."

"What is it like?" I wanted to know. She said, "I don't know. I've never gone there."

This woman was terrified. Living just a few miles from the scene of an event known the world over, she hadn't dared to venture into the fire zone herself. Yet one old fellow named Harry Truman refused to get off the mountain, even after it had shown signs of dangerous volcanic activity. He had lived there for years in his little lodge by the crystal-clear Spirit Lake. "I'm not afraid of the mountain," he said.

He should have been. We should all have a healthy fear of what can kill us. Seventy people died when Mount St. Helens erupted.

They never found a trace of Truman's body. Even several years after that eruption, most of the surface of Spirit Lake was covered by ugly, burnt trees. A shocking scene of utter devastation!

But when we look beyond the violence and upheaval of natural catastrophes, we can see another side to these events. Were it not for the ancient volcanoes, there would be no atmosphere. And probably not much vegetation, since volcanic eruptions spew chemical fertilizers throughout the world. Indeed, the natural process of recovery by the region surrounding Mount St. Helens began while the volcano still grumbled. The year after it erupted, the apple and pear crops in Oregon and Washington yielded huge surpluses. Wherever you looked, right there in the middle of the scorched earth, sprang beautiful fireweed blossoms. In a surprisingly short time, the surrounding forest of spruces and firs will be restored. It's all part of the ongoing cycle of life.

We stand appalled at the destructive force of volcanoes. But if there were no volcanoes and earthquakes, this planet would be as dead as those we see through the camera lens of the space probes. Such vital lifesigns have gradually carved and shaped the earth over millennia.

But the question still haunts us: *Why? Why couldn't we live in a "kinder, gentler" world? Does God display his awesome power without thought or mercy for its inhabitants? Couldn't God accomplish his purposes some other way?*

I don't know. I've never asked him. I'm not a god. I don't even know what it's *like* to be a god. "O the depth of the riches and wisdom and knowledge of God! How unsearchable are his judgments and how inscrutable his ways! 'For who has known the mind of the Lord, or who has been his counsellor?'" (Rom 11:33-34).

Who, indeed? God is infinite and unfathomable. We must avoid the human tendency to trivialize the very source of all light, life, and power. He is also a God of gentleness who makes little mountain gentians and delicate harebells spring out of volcanic ash; a God of beauty and splendor, even when the earth is rhythmically heaving in the throes of a violent earthquake.

If you meet anyone who doesn't believe in the Last Judgment or heaven or hell, send that poor soul to see what remains of Mount St. Helens. Right on the horizon of this unimaginable destruction, you can look up and see spectacular Mount Ranier. Yet this serene, snow-covered peak—veiled like a bride for her groom—is quite capable of becoming another huge wound in the earth just like Mount St. Helens. Things are not as they seem to be to the limited human mind.

THE HUMAN CONDITION

I use these images of utter devastation to drive home the mystery of the human condition. A terrible reality exists in this world, ready to wreak horrible destruction: *original sin*. It's not really a sin—in the sense of something you commit. We would do better to call it the *original wound* which we inherited from our first parents.

As Blaise Pascal, the French spiritual writer and philosopher, observed in his *Pensées*, each of us has a God-shaped vacuum in our hearts. This gaping hole in our souls is very much like the horrible crater left by the eruption of Mount St. Helens.

The devastation of this original wound to the human race has been incredibly violent, yet we are often too terrified or numbed to survey the scorched remains. We prefer to keep going at our daily tasks, pretending that all is well like that storekeeper near Mount St. Helens. After all, we see signs of new life stubbornly pushing through our hardened hearts. With a deep sense of foreboding, we easily ignore the warning signs of seismic activity, the deep rumbling in the very center of the human race.

When confronted by loss and suffering, we usually respond in one of two ways: *avoidance* or *denial*. We either run and hide, or we dig in our heels and ignore the evidence of impending trouble. The store clerk's refusal to set foot into the fire zone offers a clear example of avoidance. We can hear all about serious damage and even look at pictures, yet feel emotionally incapable of looking it squarely in the eye.

Harry Truman showed us what denial can do. He foolishly dug in his heels and was killed.

Those who live in a city like New York don't have to be convinced of the reality of an original wound. We "bask" in the daily smog and ashes spewed out by this human eruption. I have observed that all New Yorkers really believe in original sin, atheists included, even if they don't admit it. Unfortunately, many New Yorkers do not believe in salvation. But they all believe something is seriously wrong with this featherless biped that inhabits the uninhabitable rock of Manhattan.

What is original sin? A drama. Two people strolling hand in hand through the Garden of Eden, enjoying the bountiful produce as mere icing on the cake of their daily communion with God. Then we see them suddenly reaching for the forbidden fruit. Falling because of temptation, and in some mysterious way, transmitting that fall to their offspring.

Original sin is first of all the sin of Adam and Eve, the names given to the first human beings. Created in the image of God, they freely chose to sin against the one who had made them. As the first ancestors of the human race, they thereby lost the right to eternal life—not only for themselves, but for their offspring as well. We are all profoundly affected by the original and the actual sins of ourselves and those around us. We have all suffered enormous loss, especially in our ruptured relationship with God.

Whenever you're having a tough time, sit down and read the first few chapters of Genesis and your troubles will begin to make more sense. We see Adam and Eve, hiding in the garden, quaking in fear and shame because of their sin and nakedness. They are your parents and mine. As a fellow psychologist once said to me years ago, "We are all the victims of the victims of the victims of the victims of Adam and Eve."

Original sin also means the loss of sanctifying grace—that relationship we should have had with God at conception, but now do not. This separation from the very source of our life puts us at very grave risk in so many ways. St. Paul teaches that "sin came into the world through one man and death through sin" (Rom 5:12). Peter Kreeft talks about some of these devastating consequences in his penetrating book of apologetics, *Fundamentals of the Faith.*

> After Genesis tells the story of the good God creating a good world, it next answers the obvious question, "Where did evil come from then?" by the story of the fall of mankind. How are we to understand this? How can spiritual evil (sin) cause physical evil (suffering and death)?
> God is the source of all life and joy. Therefore, when the human soul rebels against God, it loses its life and joy. Now a human being is body as well as soul. We are single creatures, not double: we are not even body *and* soul as much as we are embodied soul, or ensouled body. So the body must share in the soul's inevitable punishment—a punishment as natural and unavoidable as broken bones from jumping off a cliff or a sick stomach from eating rotten food, rather than a punishment as artificial and external as a grade for a course, or a slap on the hands for taking the cookies.[1]

The original wound wreaks havoc in our lives similar to that of a volcanic eruption. Adam and Eve at first enjoyed a pristine garden, lush with fruits of every kind. After they deliberately disobeyed God, they suddenly had to till the barren ground in the hot sun to satisfy their hunger. Their way to the Tree of Life was forever barred, their effortless access to their maker obscured by sin.

What symptoms do we experience as a result of this original wound? Sin robs us of our right to eternal happiness, frustrating the very meaning and goal of our existence. It darkens our intellect, weakens our will, throws our emotions into chaos, and produces loneliness and alienation.

What once would have been very positive experiences have been transformed into painful, frightening, even terrifying trials. Human labor has become a burden and a curse. Begetting children has become associated with pain, sorrow, fear, and lustful exploitation. Our passage into the far better world to come—something that should have been joyous and tri-

umphant—has become fraught with sorrow. St. Paul says that
the sting of death is sin (1 Cor 15:56).

St. Augustine, that great realist, describes the human condition in desolate and terrifying terms in *The City of God*.[2] His
words should convince us of the dangers of both running and
hiding or digging in our heels and pretending nothing is wrong.

This life of ours—if a life so full of such great ills can properly
be called a life—bears witness to the fact that, from its very
start, the race of mortal men has been a race condemned.
Think, first, of that dreadful abyss of ignorance from which all
error flows and so engulfs the sons of Adam in a darksome pool
that no one can escape without the toll of toils and tears and
fears. Then, take our very love for all those things that prove so
vain and poisonous and breed so many heartaches, troubles,
griefs, and fears; such insane joys in discord, strife, and war;
such wrath and plots of enemies, deceivers, sycophants; such
fraud and theft and robbery; such perfidy and savagery, lawless-
ness and lust; all the shameless passions of the impure—fornica-
tion and adultery, incest and unnatural sins, rape and countless
other uncleannesses too nasty to be mentioned; the sins against
religion—sacrilege and heresy, blasphemy and perjury; the iniq-
uities against our neighbors—calumnies and cheating, lies and
false witness, violence to persons and property; the injustices of
the courts and the innumerable other miseries and maladies
that fill the world, yet escape attention.

It is true that it is wicked men who do such things, but the
source of all such sins is that radical canker in the mind and
will that is innate in every son of Adam. For, our infancy
proves with what ignorance of the truth man enters upon
life, and adolescence makes clear to all the world how full we
are of folly and concupiscence. In fact, if anyone were left to
live as he pleased and to do what he desired, he would go
through practically the whole gamut of lawlessnesses and
lust—those which I have just listed and, perhaps, others that
I refrained from mentioning.

Yet, for all this blight of ignorance and folly, fallen man

has not been left without some ministries of Providence, nor has God, in his anger, shut up his mercies.

DID THE CREATOR MESS IT UP?

Original sin is inextricably intertwined with the problem of evil. C.S. Lewis, the English writer who converted from atheism to the Anglican Church, was terribly troubled by this dilemma. "I did not believe that God existed. I was also very angry with him for not existing. I was also angry with him for having created the world."[3]

We constantly see good and evil locked in a terrible conflict, as graphically reflected in the tons of nuclear weapons stockpiled all around the world. Overwhelmed social welfare agencies try to protect innocent victims of appalling child abuse. The war against drugs seems to gain little ground against the incoming wave of cocaine and heroine. Today's psychotherapists face a flood of people struggling to recover from anxieties and addictions of every kind.

Why do friends turn against us? Why do our children, even when taught the finest moral values, go in the opposite direction? The answer is original sin. We cannot completely understand this mysterious spiritual principle. Yet in one way or another, original sin deeply affects our entire lives, as well as the relationships that we share with one another. It brings into human history disastrous and wicked events.

And the physical wreckage is always accompanied by spiritual thorns and thistles. The business world is littered with high-powered executives caught in greedy subterfuge. The divorce rate emphasizes the increasing estrangement between married couples. The juvenile courts cannot keep up with the deluge of young people sucked into the pit of drugs. And we are part of the problem in that we all tend to bristle in anger or wither in shame whenever someone corrects us.

If God is so good, why is the world so bad? Why do bad things happen to good people? Did God somehow botch the job of creation? Why did God give human beings free will if they were going to make such a mess out of their lives? Why couldn't the God who made the majestic mountain peaks and the most delicate rose blossoms have filled his pristine creation with sinless people, a race guaranteed not to besmudge his glorious work?

But God's creation is all good. He is not to blame for our deadly wound. We tend to think of evil as an *animated object or being*—a volcanic explosion, an earthquake, a murderous gunman. Evil has more to do with the *will*. Kreeft says, "Evil is not a thing but a wrong choice, or the damage done by a wrong choice."[4]

Let me illustrate this point by looking briefly at the life of one individual. I once saw a photograph of a quaint little house in Austria with a jagged stone inscription in front. Born into that house was a cute little baby, cuddly like all newborns. He grew to be a promising little boy—talkative, bright, outgoing, vibrant.

What happened to him? That boy became an antichrist. In that quaint house Adolf Hitler was born.

Numerous books have been dedicated to trying to understand how this one human being came to be so evil. The most convincing theories focus on Hitler's resentment of his illegitimate birth, his jealousy of others who seemed to be more talented, and his envy of Jewish students who did better in school. Hitler was particularly bitter that his German hometown had come under the rule of Austria, a fact which he called "German martyrdom." His volcanic rage may have led him to choose evil means for accomplishing his own twisted idea of a better world.

Although once a member of the church choir, Hitler had categorically rejected the church and any kind of true worship of God. Gradually descending into a deep well of hate, he eventually became capable of ordering the death of even his closest friends.

Clinical diagnostic categories and types are not designed with people like Hitler in mind—someone who seems at once a psychopathic criminal and a severely paranoid person. But even those categories pale before the shadow of Hitler's deeds.

This brings us to the next question: How are human beings

made vulnerable to such evil, to such an alliance with wickedness and the powers of darkness? Many individuals may fall as far as Hitler but are not in an historical situation to do as much damage. What about all the people who went along with Hitler's vile plans? What about those in our own country who go along with evil in our culture? The destruction of life committed in an abortion is actually based on principles first enunciated by the Nazis: "Life unworthy of life."

What about you and me? Why don't we take a stand against evil whenever we can? The answer is the absolutely devastating effects of the original wound, or to call it by its theological name, original sin. We are all accomplices to one degree or another. Don't ever trivialize life. Don't ever trivialize evil. Don't ever trivialize God. You and I are caught up in a gigantic, cosmic battle. We have a value and significance that will never pass away. We will bring it either gloriously to heaven or horribly to hell.

Faced with the awful reality of sin, many of us feel rotten about ourselves. We see our own weaknesses, our own failings, our own frightening temptations, and we become very disappointed. As a priest, I have heard the confessions of many people: ordinary and famous, peddlers and prelates, even some saintly people. I have discovered that we are *all* disappointed in ourselves—everyone, that is, except those who suffer from paranoia. That's how you can tell they're crazy! They're not disappointed in *themselves*—just in everybody else.

People are always talking about how one should have a good self-image. The man with the best self-image in the twentieth century was Adolf Hitler! The rest of us often feel miserable about ourselves. I love to hear confessions because it's a small opportunity to make people feel a little bit better about themselves through the grace of God. A saint is just a sinner who has—by the grace of God—overcome the effects of the original wound.

If you have trouble connecting with the towering image of volcanic destruction, let me suggest a smaller picture of the human condition. Imagine a tiny insect caught in a spider's web. Glittering with beads of dew on a sunny morning, the finely spun web catches an unsuspecting bug in its sticky threads. The insect can rarely free itself, even if it has the time. In fact, its vain struggles serve only to intensify the bonds which hold the insect fast.

Meanwhile, the spinner of the web is immediately alerted by unmistakable vibrations and runs to see what it has caught. To ensure another meal, the spider quickly injects the captive with enough venom to put it out of its misery. Then the killer wraps up the victim for safekeeping and returns to its observation post. No doubt another bug will soon stumble into the same trap, without even noticing the remains of the spider's previous victims.

Temptation is like the spider's web: glittering threads of evil enticements waiting to entrap those of us who foolishly pass by too closely or carelessly. Once caught in the sticky web, we are in danger of poisonous injections: lies about ourselves and our circumstances. Our entanglements in the concerns of this world can seem hopelessly complex. We can easily despair and lose hope. Slowly, we begin to fall asleep, weary of the struggle to break free.

Who can rescue us from this peril? Who can rescue us from the web of sin and hopelessness about our captivity? Where is God when we so desperately need him?

GETTING UNSTUCK

Those of us who want to grow spiritually can't go around constantly feeling rotten about ourselves or hopeless about our circumstances. Now I'm not suggesting the opposite response of always feeling just "peachy" about ourselves. Rather than being soft and fuzzy, many people have told me that I'm rather hard and prickly. My message is not that everything is just marvelous. But there is another, more realistic response to our plight than to feel rotten about ourselves. That step is personal conversion. We have to take steps to break free from the stranglehold of original sin.

This cosmic battle has been raging ever since our first parents fell. Some decades and centuries are worse than others. Isaiah predicted the birth of the Messiah in an era of peace, a feat ruth-lessly implemented by the Roman Empire. Perhaps the presence of God himself in human form also served as a potent force in keeping evil at bay—at least for a while. Yet Jesus warned his dis-ciples of impending violence and upheaval after his death.

A devout and self-educated woman mystic known as Blessed Julian of Norwich (her real name is unknown) lived through a very difficult period of history, a century before the Protestant Reformation. Born in 1342, she was an anchoress, a holy woman who lived alone in a little cell at the entrance to a country church in northern England. During her lifetime, twenty-five million people died from the Black Death in just two years. The plague killed one-third of the population from Turkey to Iceland.

Several priests at that time led the peasants in a revolution for human rights. Near where Julian lived, a diocesan priest was executed by a particularly excruciating method. His limbs were tied to wild horses which were then sent in opposite directions. His dismembered body was then carried to the corners of the realm to frighten the peasants into submission.

Do such violent expressions of our human condition seem shocking? I am sure we could find even greater horrors in our own century. The Nazi camps of Auschwitz and Dachau may top the list in demonstrating gross disregard for human dignity and worth. The deaths of millions of babies dismembered in their mothers' wombs every year are a daily affront to God's goodness. Unfortunately, the human race has not become more civilized in the spiritual sense. Its wound has only festered and grievously infected all of creation in every age.

Julian herself suffered from a very serious illness in 1373, dur-ing which she experienced what she called "showings." These pri-vate revelations are certainly not the work of the Holy Spirit in the same way as the Scriptures, but they are nonetheless very interest-ing and enlightening. Here is Blessed Julian's very powerful para-ble about a hapless servant sent on an errand by his master:

> I saw two persons in bodily form, a lord and a servant.... The
> lord is seated in solemn state, at rest and at peace. The servant

is standing by his lord respectfully, ready to do his master's will. With love, gracious and tender, the lord looks on his servant, and sends him on an errand to a certain place. Not only does the servant go, but he darts off at once, running at great speed, for love's sake, to do his master's bidding. Almost at once he falls into a ditch and hurts himself badly. He moans and groans, cries out and struggles, but he cannot get up or help himself in any way. Yet as I saw it, his greatest trial was that there was no one to comfort at hand; for he was unable so much as to turn his face to look upon his loving lord, in whom is full comfort; and this, although he was very close to him. Instead, behaving weakly and foolishly for time being, he thought only of his grief and distress.

In his plight he suffered several great pains. First, there was the severe bruising from the fall, and this hurt him greatly; secondly, there was the sheer weight of his body; thirdly, there was the weakness that followed from these two; fourthly, he was severely shocked and stunned, so that he had almost forgotten his own love; in the fifth place, he was unable to get up. The sixth pain was to me extraordinary, for this was that he lay all alone. I looked and searched all round, but far or near, high or low, I could see no one to help him. And the last pain was that he lay in a lonely place, narrow, rough and forbidding.

I marvelled how this servant could meekly suffer such distress, and I looked carefully to see if I could discover any fault in him, or if his master should assign any blame. But I saw none: for the only cause of his fall was his good will and his eagerness. He was now in spirit just as willing and good as when he stood before his lord ready to do his will.[5]

Does this servant's plight sound at all familiar? When we ourselves fall into serious sin, our physical agonies often seem magnified by our helplessness. We are sure God is horrified at our behavior, even though we started out our journey with such good intentions. Anyway, who had the audacity to dig this ditch right in the middle of the broad highway? A grand "pity party" usually ensues, as we complain and blame others for our misery. Our common wound quickly festers into "terminal uniqueness," where we feel alone and out of the reach of God's saving grasp.

Yet, in the midst of our groaning, how is the Lord really looking upon us? Is he full of condemnation as we seem to assume? Let's continue with the parable of Blessed Julian:

> His loving lord, now tenderly looking upon his servant, regards him in two ways. First, outwardly, very lovingly and gently, with great compassion and pity.... Then secondly... I saw the lord greatly rejoicing in the thought of the deserved rest and high honor he will surely bestow on his servant in his bounteous grace.... It was as though this courteous lord had said, "See my beloved servant here, what hurt and distress he has endured in the service of love of me—and of his good will. Is it not fitting that I should reward him for his fright and fear, his pain and his wounds, and all his grief? And not only this. Should I not award him a gift which would serve him better, and be more excellent than his own health would have been? Surely, it would be most ungracious of me if I did not do this."... I saw that it must indeed be by virtue of his lord's great worth and goodness, that his beloved servant, whom he loves so dearly, should be truly and happily rewarded, beyond all that would have been if he had not fallen. Yes, and yet more, that his falling, and his grief which he has taken upon himself, should be turned into surpassing glory and endless joy.
>
> I understood that the lord who sat there in stately rest and peace was God. The servant... was Adam; thus one man was shown as falling at a particular time, to make it clear how God regards all men and their falling. For in the sight of God all men stand for one man, for one Man stands for all men. This man was hurt in the day of his strength and was made very weak; and he was stunned in his mind so that he looked away from his lord. But his will was kept constant in God's sight; for I saw the lord commend and approve his will, but he, himself, was hindered and blinded from knowing his own will; and this

causes him great sorrow and grief; for neither does he see clearly his loving lord, who is to him so gentle and humble, nor does he see truly what he is in himself in the sight of his gracious lord. And I know well that when these two things are wisely and truly seen, we shall have rest and peace in part in this life, and by his bounteous grace, the fullness of joy in heaven.

... I saw that pain alone blames and punishes, and that our courteous lord comforts and succours, ever bringing gladness and joy to the soul, loving and longing to bring us to his own blessedness.[6]

It is obvious that Julian is not writing directly about Adam as the first parent of the human race, but about any person of good will who falls into serious sin. *You and I are the ones stuck in that ditch and the loving Lord is the one who comes to help us.*

How desperately we need to know that God is right by our side, loving us even when we feel lost and forsaken. Yet we so often lose sight of our loving Savior. Or even worse, we purposely hide from God, when only his love can rescue us. Remember Adam and Eve in the garden, who immediately clothed their naked bodies and hid when they heard God calling. They feared his anger instead of trusting in his love.

And how often we hide our shame from one another. The tendency is observable even in children. A young girl who has been sexually molested by the apparently kindly older man next door, is absolutely incapable of understanding her pitiful plight. Filled with shame, she feels utterly abandoned. Her childish perspective places the blame squarely on her own little shoulders. What did she do to invite this man to touch her that way? Fearing her parents' anger instead of trusting in their love, this innocent victim cannot bring herself to tell them—perhaps the only people who can protect her from further damage.

Who will rescue us from the deadly ditches deepened by our own fears? An important tenet of the Catholic faith is that there is *always* hope of salvation until a person has finally passed the frontier of death. God predestines no one to hell. Even the worst of sinners may yet be saved through the mercy and goodness of God. He does not wish the death of sinners, but their salvation. In fact, God relentlessly pursues us with the burning jealousy of a spurned lover.

Nonetheless, we all go around with the suspicion that we ourselves are hopeless. A few days before his death, even St. Francis of Assisi was asking the friars to pray that he wouldn't be lost! At times you and I are convinced we are the worst of sinners. Yet most of us have received an immense amount of grace. We have received the Christian faith and the grace to keep it alive. We have received the sacraments.

Knowing that we have been heaped with grace upon grace upon grace inevitably can make us feel like even worse sinners. We have all received so much and yet given so small a return. From those who have received much, much is expected. I have received the Body and Blood of Christ almost every day since I began high school. "How much have you given?" will be asked of me at the Judgment—and rightly so.

A London newspaper once invited various popular writers to submit articles for a series about "what's wrong with the world?" G.K. Chesterton, the Catholic apologist, submitted the following letter:

Gentlemen,
I am.
Sincerely yours,
G.K. Chesterton

Most thinking Christians feel the same way about themselves. What's wrong with the world? *They are!* We are! Many others seem to have lost any sense of sin. Modern pop-psychology has successfully convinced many that the experience of guilt is merely an unhealthy habit to be avoided at all costs. Yet the Holy Spirit is constantly at work in our hearts to convince us of the need to struggle against our tendency of rebellion against God.

Many remain unaware all their lives of the full gravity of sin. Indeed, who among us could even begin to glimpse the cataclysmic reality? Even in our ignorance, we often intuitively feel that all is not well in the deepest part of our being.

Not one of us would have any hope of salvation at all if it depended completely on us. If a person had to be *worthy* of salvation, even the Virgin Mary would not be saved. She was saved in a different way than the rest of us—by the Immaculate Conception—but she was saved nonetheless by the grace of Christ.

All of us, every child of Adam and Eve, in some incomprehensibly mysterious way was born into a spiritual reality that makes Mount St. Helens look like a firecracker. God's exquisite creation has become a place of utter devastation and death.

THE PITY OF GOD

Adam and Eve had suffered a grievous fall. Yet right there in Genesis, on the very occasion of the first sin, we are told that God promised a Redeemer. The saving promise of grace was given. Why? *Because God is filled with pity.*

We sometimes catch a glimpse of the divine pity in the death of our Savior, especially in the beautiful image of the Sacred Heart of Jesus. We are reminded through Our Lady that God lifted a human being so high that she became the embodiment of gentle pity and maternal forgiveness. But we don't think enough about the pity of God. Blessed Julian ends her vision with these words:

His countenance was merciful. His face finely featured, olive-colored brown. His eyes were dark, soft and peaceful, filled with deep and tender compassion, revealing him to be a sure and ample refuge embracing the fullness of heaven. For of the gracious look continually bestowed upon his servant, especially in his falling, it seemed to me that it could melt our hearts for love and break them for love. For in his lovely gaze it was a blend of qualities beautiful to see. On the one hand, compassion and pity. On the other hand, blessedness and joy.

The blessedness and joy surpassed the compassion and pity. The pity belongs to earth; the blessedness belongs to heaven.[7]

God is full of compassion, always looking for some way to reach the lost and forsaken. Don't try to understand *how* God will save somebody else. Cardinal John Henry Newman pointed out that the grace that suits one person is not the grace that suits another. We have no right to say how and when and where God will lead another person to salvation. The ways by which perfection is reached reflect infinite variety. Our wounded souls require very different medicines. God can even lead a person by means of his or her weakness and sin. Haven't we all marveled at how he can bring good out of evil?

During this past year, I have known many people dying of AIDS. Yet many victims of this painful and disastrous illness die prayerfully, with their hearts and minds open to God. Somehow they receive the grace to accept the bitterness of a short life which has ended in such an apparently meaningless way.

This awful disease is sometimes passed on by immoral behavior—perhaps sexual promiscuity or drug addiction. Do you think that stops God? *God is always there*. He goes to the hospital, to the prison, to the crackhouse. He even goes down into the darkest and blackest heart and calls that person to himself, because he is filled with pity. He came to save sinners, not the self-righteous. I somehow think God frequents a place of drugs or prostitution as often as he does a church or retreat. Where are the cries of anguish likely to be the most heart-rending?

The Catholic faith teaches that all human beings have original sin, but that it does not totally destroy their goodness. It is a *wound*, a deadly poison for which God has provided an antidote. It hampers us, inhibits us. When left to ourselves, original sin causes us to lose our salvation. But something good remains. As Blessed Julian said in her vision, the glorious Lord seated on his throne could look over to that bruised and battered servant and be filled not with indignation, but with pity.

Julian's vision is a powerful pictorial representation of the words of Jesus when he says, "Come to me, all who labour and are heavy laden, and I will give you rest. Take my yoke upon you, and learn from me; for I am gentle and lowly in heart, and you will find rest for your souls. For my yoke is easy, and my burden is light" (Mt 11:28-30).

Anyone who is aware of his or her own weakness and sinfulness must always remember that Jesus came not to call the righteous, but sinners, to repentance (Lk 5:31-32). The Good Shepherd comes to seek and to find the lost lambs. He leaves the ninety-nine who are safe and goes in search of the one who has gone astray. "So it is not the will of my Father who is in heaven that one of these little ones should perish" (Mt 18:14).

How can we ever understand the pity of God? His infinite goodness and mercy is found in the fall of the human race. Something made him want to save us. Perhaps it was our utter inability to rescue ourselves. How does a mother respond to her newborn infant who cries out with hunger? Does she send the baby to the nearest grocery store with a dollar bill? No, she tenderly picks up her child and provides milk.

God knows how dependent we are on his grace, literally for every breath we draw. He never gives up on us, never turns his back on us. God is always there for us, calling us to himself. No sinner is beyond his reach. But God may use each of us to reach out to one of his lost lambs on his behalf. Let's consider the story of one mother who watched her grown child fall into a pit of shame and confusion.

DRENCHED WITH TEARS

Once when I was on business in Rome for a couple of days, I got up very early and went on a little pilgrimage of nearby churches. I was staying at the Casa Santa Maria, in the center of the old section of Rome. I first offered Mass at the tomb of St. Aloysius Gonzaga in the Church of St. Ignatius. Then I went to the church named Santa Maria Sopra Minerva, where St. Catherine of Siena and Blessed Angelico are buried.

Finally, almost irresistibly, my steps took me to a very old church, on the side of which is a small chapel with a tomb—the burial place of a woman who died in Rome sixteen hundred years ago. I paused there a long time to pray and think about St. Monica. Lovely frescoes decorate the walls of the chapel. One shows her weeping and being consoled by a bishop. When he asked Monica why she was crying, the distraught woman answered, "I'm crying for my son." The bishop said, "Don't worry. The son of these tears will not be lost."[8]

Her son had his own ideas. As a matter of fact, his rebellion worsened year after year. Rather than cooperating with the grace of God, he angrily rebuked the mother who reached out to him in the love of God. Did this stop Monica? Not for an instant.

Not only was her son a serious concern, Monica was married to an abusive husband as well. Instead of drowning in her own sorrow, this saintly woman never stopped praying for both of her loved ones. Shortly after his baptism Monica's husband became ill, and was well-prepared for death. God also answered Monica's prayers for her son, and we know him as St. Augustine. God heard this wonderful woman's tearful prayers—the prayers of a lifetime, the prayers of a persistent widow and mother.

Jesus told his disciples a parable of persisting in prayer and not losing heart:

In a certain city there was a judge who neither feared God nor regarded man; and there was a widow in that city who kept coming to him and saying, "Vindicate me against my adversary." For a while he refused; but afterward he said to himself, "Though I neither fear God nor regard man, yet because this widow bothers me, I will vindicate her, or she will wear me out by her continual coming."

And the Lord said, "Hear what the unrighteous judge says. And will not God vindicate his elect, who cry to him day and night? Will he delay long over them? I tell you, he will vindicate them speedily. Nevertheless, when the Son of man comes, will he find faith on earth?" Lk 18:2-8

How important it is for us to take this parable of our Lord seriously. He is not telling us that God is an unjust judge. He is telling us to be *persistent*. All sorts of things go wrong in the world that are not the will of God. There is an immense difference between the *actual* will of God which decrees events and the *permissive* will of God which allows them. The actual will of God caused the incarnation. The permissive will of God allowed the crucifixion to take place—the best and the worst of all human events. We need to recall that whatever happens, God goes with us. God was there at the crucifixion as much as he was there at the resurrection.

As I gazed at the murals in the chapel of St. Monica, I thought how much this mother is like so many of us. I'm sure there were many times when this poor woman wondered if anyone cared. Her husband was a pagan for years. Her son was worse than a pagan. These loved ones probably considered her a religious fanatic, a bother, a busybody. Hardly anyone else paid much attention, except for two bishops who were moved to compassion by her prayers.

Meanwhile, Monica became one of the first people to receive Holy Communion daily. In her time, Mass was not said in all churches every day, only on Sundays, Holy Days, and at funerals. Monica apparently would get hold of the obituary from the town crier and make it to a funeral every day. She would make a circuit of different churches to make sure she attended the liturgy.[9]

Monica is a saint of prayer, a saint of tears. Her symbol is a handkerchief. If you see a statue of a woman holding a handkerchief, that's old Monica. This devout mother didn't think her son gave a hoot—and most of the time he probably didn't. But out of the corner of his eye, the rebellious and stubborn young man must have watched the old lady.

Only a few months before her death, Augustine told his mother of his conversion. "She was filled with triumphant exultation, and praised you, O Lord, who are mighty beyond what we ask or conceive: for she saw that you had given her more than with all her pitiful weeping she had ever asked. You had converted me to yourself...."[10]

Augustine himself would become one of the great composers of prayers in church history—a man who had sought out the darkness, sinking deeper and deeper into the pit. But because his mother had prayed without ceasing for years, St. Augustine could say to the Lord, "Flood our path with your light when the road is long and the way is weary and let us know of your presence."

Who taught him to pray? A woman who ten thousand times must have said, "My God, my God, why have you forsaken me?" Yet God's word poignantly reminds us that he is filled with pity and compassion. "Can a woman forget her sucking child, that she should have no compassion on the son of her womb? Even these may forget you, yet I will not forget you. Behold, I have graven you on the palms of my hands..." (Is 49:15-16).

Even if the woman who bore you and nurtured you should forget you, God will never lose sight of you. The proof of his love and compassion is printed with nails in the palms of his only Son, Jesus Christ.

EVEN SPIRITUAL PEOPLE GET DEPRESSED

If you think you're going to be a spiritual person and not go through very dark times, you're sadly mistaken. After I had just spoken on this very subject at a conference, I was called to the phone. A desperate priest was crying out for help—a devout, generous, dedicated man who suffers from deep depression.

Like anybody battling that kind of affliction, he had become desperate. Most of us, sooner or later, feel that everything is lost. We often beat ourselves to death with pain, shame, and guilt, especially if we take our spiritual lives seriously.

Christ has given us a prayer to be said in such dark times—a prayer so startling that we wouldn't believe that he said it, were it not recorded in the Bible. As Jesus hung on the cross in agony, he cried out with a loud voice, *"My God, my God, why hast thou forsaken me?"* (Mt 27:46). What did Jesus do in the midst of utter darkness? He did exactly what he had told other people to do. Jesus said, "Take heed, watch and pray; for you do not know when the time [of tribulation] will come" (Mk 13:33).

Why did Jesus cry out these words to his Father? Had God forsaken his Son? No! But the human spirit, the human life, the human will and mind of even the Messiah himself must have been overwhelmed by an utter sense of loneliness, desperation, and dereliction.

Jesus was not giving up hope. He was actually praying the first line of Psalm 22, to me an astoundingly precise prophecy of the crucifixion. His wrenching cry to the Lord was not one of despair, but that of one who knows God will come to save and deliver. "In thee our fathers trusted; they trusted, and thou didst deliver them. To thee they cried, and were saved; in thee they trusted, and were not disappointed" (Ps 22:4-5).

We begin to grow only when we know that prayer intimately from the inside. When we can pray from the depths of our hearts, "My God, my God, why have you forsaken me?" I have known many people who could say only that one prayer. I have had days in my own life when I could say only that prayer. It is, as it were, the last prayer in the book. Most of us will say it sooner or later.

"Why have you forsaken me?" That is the prayer of ultimate love. Not our love for God. God's love *for us* and *to us* is revealed in that cry which comes from the heart of the dying Messiah.

St. John of the Cross said, "I saw that there was a river that every soul must cross who would come to the kingdom of heaven. The name of that river is sorrow and the boat on which we cross it is called love." And love does not permit us to fail. Why do we forget time and again that God loves us?

The reason for his love is not in ourselves, but in God's way of seeing us. Our heavenly Father looks upon us as his little children, much the way parents love and delight in their newborn offspring. A little baby can perform no great feats, but rather, requires a good deal of care and support. Do the parents begrudge what this little creature so freely consumes? Of course not. We must never forget that God feels the same way about us. God saves us because he loves us.

The journey can seem painfully long. When a year is coming to an end, we may think back over the months and say, "Well, it wasn't too bad." People rarely look back and gush, "That was a great year!" Sometimes, but not very often, and I don't trust the people who say it. More often we say, "This one wasn't too bad. It rose to the glorious level of a C-plus."

And after the worst ones, we can usually say, "Well, it's got to get better. Statistically, it can't stay this bad."

So we gather up the hope and courage to trudge forward. Perhaps the years that accomplish the most for our spiritual lives are precisely the long, dull ones. Like St. Augustine, we need to cry out to our loving Father to flood our paths with light, because even in our darkest nights, he is listening.

I began this chapter with the tragic story of Betty. I still see her children and grandchildren during the holidays and whenever they have a particular need. I still think of her funeral when I drive past the old church or Mount Sinai Hospital. Betty's family has demonstrated the strength and courage to persevere through difficulty and sorrow. They can laugh; they struggle to do a little bit better, and they keep their eyes on the world to come. This is the strength and wisdom of the poor.

Those who work with the poor can recognize these qualities regardless of the particular race or culture. Unfortunately, wealth, leisure, and ease often separate people from this strength and wisdom. The irony is that spiritually, the rich can suffer a great deal more because they lack these qualities. I am grateful to God that I have worked with the poor most of my life. From them I have learned a lot about how to trust in God and keep going.

An elderly black woman summed it up very well when she came to pick up a box of food. She faced many problems and had known much sorrow. I asked her, "Please pray for me." She looked at me very directly and replied, "Father, if I didn't pray always, I could never keep going."

◆ ◆ ◆

Oh Jesus, you who experienced and shared this devastated world with us, we trust you to be with us in the dark times. At moments, life can be beautiful and fulfilling; at others, it can be like a hell. Often, its dullness only leaves us weary.

But your Holy Spirit whispers in our hearts that you are here with us. You are not put off by our faults, our ingratitude, our weakness, even our sinfulness. You look upon us like lost sheep, like the prodigal son. You look upon us with pity and not with blame. You do not cause us to be lost, but rather to be saved. We cause our own loss if we refuse to turn to you.

Hold onto my hand in the darkness. Come to me in the lonely night. Guide me through the rough places. Help others who come to me to find your loving presence. Assure us all by your Holy Spirit that you are always there for us, O merciful Savior. Amen.

TWO

Hope in the Midst of Hell: Our Justification

Come to me, all who labor and are heavy laden, and I will give you rest. Take my yoke upon you, and learn from me; for I am gentle and lowly in heart, and you will find rest for your souls. Mt 11:28-29

DURING THE FINAL DAYS of World War II, the prisoners at Dachau heard a very frightening rumor: Hitler had ordered the execution of all prisoners and the burning of all concentration camps. Day after day the emaciated men and women could hear the sound of nearby artillery fire and bombs falling on Munich. When all the guards suddenly fled, the terrified prisoners believed that the camp was about to be bombed as well.

Certain of doom, these pitiful victims prepared for death. Finally, they heard tanks approach and surround the camp. One began slamming into the main gate. It backed up and slammed again until the gate crashed to the ground. The prisoners cowered in terror, too exhausted to move.

Then a miracle! Through the gate came a tank with an American flag painted on its front. With what little strength they had left, the stunned survivors sent up a cheer. They had been saved! The next day they joined in a Mass of thanksgiving. The principal celebrant was an eighty-four-year-old Lithuanian priest who had also been a prisoner for over four years.

As the gate was ripped from its hinges, a sign was exposed which had secretly been painted underneath the lintel by some prisoner doing a repair job. Four letters in white: *spes*, the Latin word for *hope*. These wretched human beings had been utterly condemned, as good as dead. How did they manage to hold onto any sense of hope in this hellhole? Was that prisoner a priest, since the sign was in Latin?

Tears came to my eyes when my dear friend, Monsignor Arthur Rojeck, told me of his liberation from Dachau. As a Polish military chaplain, he had been imprisoned in concentration camps for over four years, first at Auschwitz and Birkenau, and then, Dachau. He had witnessed the martyrdom of St. Maximilian Kolbe at Auschwitz and believed his own death was imminent.

Although the Jews suffered mass extermination, they weren't the only victims of Hitler. One out of every ten prisoners who died at Dachau was a Catholic priest—three thousand in all. Fr. Rojeck himself was tortured and beaten. A tall man with a large frame, he weighed a mere sixty-six pounds, was extremely emaciated, and only a few days from death by starvation at the end of his captivity.

What a dramatic story of *deliverance!* The destiny of the prisoners at Dachau seemed sealed. In the worst possible circumstances, they had no fight left in them and were waiting to die. Suddenly they were set free to live again.

ADRIFT ON A VAST SEA

An even greater deliverance has rescued the entire human race, yet those of us born into the faith and baptized as infants seldom spend much time thinking about this tremendous reality.

Pondering it could transform our lives. How desperately we need an eternal perspective to see us through our private hellholes!

What does deliverance mean? Another word for this aspect of our salvation is *justification*. The Council of Trent says, "Justification is the transition from that condition in which man is born as the son of the first Adam into the state of grace and adoption among the children of God through the second Adam, Jesus Christ our Savior." St. Bonaventure, the great mystic, eloquently described it this way:

> In the initial state of creation, man was made fit for the quiet of contemplation, and therefore God placed him in a paradise of delights (Gn 2:15). But turning from the true light to changeable good, man was bent over by his own fault, and the entire human race by original sin, which infected human nature in two ways: the mind with ignorance and the flesh with concupiscence. As a result, man, blinded and bent over, sits in darkness and does not see the light of heaven unless grace with justice come to his aid against concupiscence and unless knowledge with wisdom come to his aid against ignorance. All this is done through Jesus Christ, whom God made for us wisdom, justice, sanctification and redemption (1 Cor 1:30). Since he is the power of God and the wisdom of God (1 Cor 1:24), the incarnate Word full of grace and truth (Jn 1:14), he made grace and truth. That is, he pours out the grace of charity, which, since it flows from a pure heart and a good conscience and faith unfeigned (1 Tm 1:5), rectifies the entire soul in the threefold orientation mentioned above.[1]

We described original sin in the last chapter as an awful wound inherited from our first parents. What is St. Bonaventure saying here? That we were created to enjoy God's presence, to bask in the light of his glory. Yet we turned away from that light and turned in on ourselves. Rather than obey their Creator, Adam and Eve were tempted to taste transitory enticements.

Human flesh desired the knowledge of good and evil apart from God, wisdom apart from the eternal source of truth.

The effects of this rebellion were disastrous for us all: sin, death, ignorance, darkness. We sit in shadows, unable to see the light of heaven except by the grace of God. We are doomed to eternal darkness unless God delivers us from condemnation. We will rot in our own ignorance unless God gives us wisdom from above.

How often we fail to recognize our dire straits. The analogy that comes to my mind would be almost comical were the danger not so great. Picture some happy campers packing up their gear, refreshed after a few days in the wilderness. To their distress, the campfire they thought had been sufficiently snuffed out begins to flare up again. As they douse the flames, a small brush fire begins to blaze across the way. "What a bother!" they think, anxious to get moving. Little do they realize that just over the ridge, a forest fire is raging out of control. Their only escape route no longer exists.

How often do we find ourselves so busy trying to snuff out the brush fires of temptation, while unaware of the savage firestorm of evil swirling perilously nearby? But God has *not* left us to die. He has mercifully sent his own Son, Jesus Christ, to deliver us from the raging fire of sin and its awful effects.

Why do many of us rarely pause to think about our deliverance, that Jesus came to save this fallen world from darkness and certain death? Perhaps you were raised as a Catholic. You may have prayed fervently since you were a young child. Perhaps you have been a daily communicant. Being so close to the great truths of our salvation can sometimes blind us to the magnitude of God's mercy.

On the other hand, perhaps you have spent years separated from God, never thinking about him, never praying. You may have struggled with terrible personal problems like alcoholism or bankruptcy or cancer. You may remember a time when you yourself sat in shadows, unable to see the light. Often those who have fallen away from the practice of faith return to a clearer sense of deliverance than those who have always tried to be faithful.

But really, we are all in the same boat. We are all like those throngs of boat people escaping despots, refugees afloat on a very big ocean, hoping a storm doesn't blow up and capsize our flimsy craft. Some of us just don't realize it. We may *feel* relatively safe and secure—as if we were aboard a yacht equipped with enough food and lifeboats to ensure our survival, even a radio to call for help in case disaster should strike.

Are we really so safe and secure as we sometimes think? Many of us could not face another day if we really knew how precarious our situation was. Apart from God's mercy, we are like drowning persons going down for the third time, with no rescue in sight. Jesus Christ has saved us from certain death. Stop and think about it. Send up a cheer to God like those dying prisoners at Dachau.

I very much appreciate the way Peter Kreeft describes deliverance in *Fundamentals of the Faith*. He says we find safety and security only when we are "washed in the blood of the Lamb."

Love wants to be inside the beloved; love wants exchange. Thus God exchanged his deliverance for our evil, his garbage truck for our garbage. What happened on the cross is no freak accident, no exception, but the universal principle of what love does. Love delivers the beloved from evil by taking it upon itself and soaking it up, like a blotter.

It is a bloody business, deliverance. Where do we find deliverance? There, in Christ's wounds. Remember the line of the great old (forgotten?) prayer "Anima Christi": "In thy wounds hide me." The devil dare not come there. He cringes from the blood. That is the safest place to be.... Our deliverance is to be "washed in the blood of the Lamb."[2]

Picture a group of impoverished refugees afloat in a rickety boat. Suddenly a huge ocean liner appears on the horizon. The captain spots the small craft and mercifully takes the pitiful pilgrims aboard. He lavishes them with kindness, tends to their wounds, feeds them delicious food, clothes them in fine garments, and gives them soft beds in which to sleep.

Yet the owner of the vessel is not content with this generosity. After they have been refreshed, he visits them with some astounding news. He has just legally adopted this motley crew into his own family! Completely undeserving, they are now joint heirs of his whole estate!

Does such a story sound totally preposterous? That's exactly what has happened to us in Jesus Christ. God has personally reached down and plucked each one of us out of the ocean. We may have still been bravely swimming—no doubt warily eyeing the circling sharks. Or we may have already exhausted our own strength and been perilously close to drowning. Either way, we were all doomed without having been personally rescued by the only person capable of such a mighty deliverance: God himself in the person of his only Son.

Justification accomplishes such a work in each of our lives— *not only the remission of sin but also the sanctification and reno- vation of the inner person.* To be justified means to be made right with God. Because of sin, we had been condemned to death. Yet Jesus paid our debt by dying on the cross. But justi- fication does not make one saved and immediately ready to enter into eternal glory. Because we have been so devastated by the original wound, God sends his Holy Spirit into our hearts to heal and transform us.

The Reformers did not agree with this understanding of jus- tification. They believed that the human being remained cor- rupt—"totally depraved," in Calvin's words—but that grace was poured over the soul so that we could be saved. They saw justification as kind of an outer coating—sort of an Eskimo pie in reverse.

Martin Luther was a crusty old fellow given to colorful expressions—sort of like myself, I'm afraid. He used a graphic German expression to describe human nature as saved by grace, which means "a manure pile covered with snow." That was Luther's idea of the saved person. I must admit, I sometimes feel like that myself. Haunted by neurotic guilt, young Luther knew he could never do enough good works to be saved. It finally dawned on this passionate, intelligent, and somewhat pessimistic man that indeed he had already been justified, that he did not need to depend on his good works which he had taken too seriously.

The Fathers of the Council of Trent understood this truth of our salvation differently. They said that justification was, rather, the *renewal* of fallen human nature. Some people just don't happen to *look* very renewed. Even though our hearts have already been made new in Christ, our transformation is an ongoing process that takes a lot of time. Let's face it. We all have piled up a lot of manure over the years. Some of us just manage to hide it better than others.

THE WORST OF SINNERS

Adolf Hitler is often held up as the epitome of evil, ultimately responsible for the torture and death of millions of Jews and other innocent victims. Joseph Stalin collaborated with the Allies to defeat Germany, all the while ordering the execution of thousands of Polish officers in preparation for a Communist takeover. He also ordered the death by starvation of eleven million Ukranians.

Were either Hitler or Stalin beyond the reach of God to save? One of the important teachings of the Catholic Church is that when Christ died, he potentially saved *every* human being who has ever walked this earth. The Catholic Church teaches that no child is born predestined to hell. Anyone is capable of being called to salvation because Christ came to save the entire human race. The most wretched sinner in the world can be saved, even a Hitler or a Stalin if he were to repent.

St. Paul himself laid claim to the distinction of being the worst sinner: "The saying is sure and worthy of full acceptance, that Christ Jesus came into the world to save sinners. And I am the foremost of sinners; but I received mercy for this reason, that in me, as the foremost, Jesus Christ might display his perfect patience for an example to those who were to believe in him for eternal life" (1 Tm 1:15-16).

Saul of Tarsus, known to us as St. Paul, was a determined enemy of Christ, a violent persecutor of the early Christians, a proud witness of the martyrdom of Stephen. Having petitioned the high priest for letters to the synagogues at Damascus, this zealot was on his way to find more Christians to deliver bound to Jerusalem. While Saul was breathing murderous threats against the first Christian believers, the risen Jesus came to this foremost of sinners and personally revealed the light of heaven to him.

God had mercy on Saul because he loved him and had pity on his fallen state. After he had accomplished a great work of deliverance and justification in Paul's heart and mind, the Lord also sent him to preach the good news to the Gentiles.

We can learn something from another man who could be considered a terrible sinner in our own century. He killed an eleven-year-old girl, Maria Goretti, who was canonized a saint forty-five years after her death. Maria was the third of six children born to an impoverished family in Italy. After her father died of malaria, she worked generously and cheerfully to help her widowed mother.

Maria's family shared a farmhouse with Giovanni Serenelli and his son, Alessandro. The father sought relief from his poverty through alcohol; both he and his son amused themselves with pornographic magazines. About a month before the murder, Alessandro began making lustful advances to Maria. While her mother was busy in the fields one day, he ordered the young girl to mend one of his shirts. Suddenly Alessandro grabbed her and threatened her with a knife, demanding that she submit to him.

Maria refused to yield, protesting that to do so would be a sin against God. In a rage, Alessandro stabbed her fourteen times in her heart, lungs, and intestines. When her mother found her mortally wounded on the kitchen floor, the murderer was in his room, pretending to be asleep.

Taken to the hospital, Maria lay in excruciating pain for twenty hours. She spent her last hours praying and forgiving her assailant, asking that this evil man be with her one day in heaven. Alessandro was tried for murder and sentenced to thirty years in prison. While still in prison, he finally repented of his sins after he claimed that Maria appeared to him in a vision with an armful of lilies. After he accepted them, each flower was transformed into a still, white flame.

Alessandro Serenelli lived a life of profound darkness, degeneration, godlessness, hopelessness, and negativism. But after his conversion, he led a very devout life—the last twenty with the Capuchins as a penitent.

No one is beyond salvation. You couldn't say even to Hitler or Stalin, "It's too late. You've done it all. There's no forgiveness for you."

The Catholic Church so desires *everyone* to be saved that when she excommunicates someone due to a most serious and scandalous sin, she does so not to condemn, but hopefully to bring the person to repentance. *Any* excommunication can be absolved. As a matter of fact, any priest can absolve any excommunication at the hour of death—even if the priest himself has left the Catholic Church and renounced the priesthood. All limitations are over at the hour of death because the "supreme law is the salvation of souls."

Is there someone you know who doesn't look like he or she is bound for glory? We all have loved ones who as far as we can tell haven't said a prayer in years. Remember that Jesus Christ died on the cross for them, just as he died on the cross for St. Mary Magdalen and the Good Thief. On Calvary there stood the most innocent mother of Jesus and Mary Magdalen, John the Apostle, and the Good Thief—representing the range of humanity. The salvation of all human beings was potentially accomplished. Of course, each person must make his or her own step to receive the grace of Christ when it is offered. This is what we call justification. *An individual person is justified when he or she turns to God by faith.*

THE OLD ARGUMENT

Here's where a long-standing debate flares up about justification. St. Paul says the just person shall live by *faith* (Rom 1:17). Many Protestants believe in *faith alone*, while Catholics and Orthodox Christians believe in *faith and works*—or so the old argument goes. Maybe. I was speaking at an evangelical convention in Honolulu a couple of years ago. Eighteen hundred people were in attendance, seventeen hundred of them evangelical Protestants.

I said to them, "I think the whole argument over faith and works was drummed up as an argument of words at the time of the Reformation, so that the Protestants and Catholics would have something to yell back and forth at each other." Throughout the audience I saw people nodding in agreement. An eminent evangelical theologian got up later and said the same thing.

Did you ever meet any Catholics who thought they could be saved by doing good works if they didn't have faith? No. Did you ever meet any Catholics who thought that by doing good works they would be saved, apart from the grace of our Lord Jesus Christ? No. Did you ever meet a devout, believing Protestant who didn't do good works? No. So there must be something wrong with the argument.

The entire human race was set right with God, or saved, by the coming of our Lord Jesus Christ who is our justification. It is untrue to say that we are saved either by faith or by works, or by faith and works together. *We are saved by Jesus Christ.* He alone is the cause of our salvation. We are saved by a person and not by belief in any doctrine. Our lives are enlightened, touched, and justified when we put our *faith* in him.

The New Testament makes it eminently clear that only Jesus has the power to undo the effects of original sin. Jesus is our Savior. Without him, we have absolutely no hope of salvation. His life and death were the sacrifice by which we were set right with God.

Granted, absurd abuses raged among Catholics at the time of the Reformation. Some believers thought they could be saved by giving donations, especially to the building of St. Peter's in Rome. Certain idiots were going around selling indulgences that supposedly guaranteed entry into heaven. Many a crook over the centuries has decided to make a little money on religion. That's nothing new, nor are abuses limited to the Catholic Church and the fifteenth century. In our own times, we have often seen the gospel used to cheat people.

St. Augustine faced this argument eyeball to eyeball. Baptized believers who were living licentious lives would say, "We've been saved. We don't have to behave. We can do whatever we want. How wonderfully liberating!" St. Augustine referred them to the Epistle of St. James: "Show me your faith apart from your works, and I by my works will show you my faith" (Jas 2:18). For a person to enter into the life of grace, it is necessary for their faith to be manifested through good works.

Dr. Peter Kreeft, a convert to Catholicism, recalls being taught that Catholics believed in faith through good works. He writes: "I remember vividly the thrill of discovery when, as a young Protestant at Calvin College, I read St. Thomas Aquinas and the Council of Trent on justification. I did not find what I had been told I would find, 'another gospel' of do-it-yourself salvation by works, but a clear and forceful statement that we can do nothing without God's grace, and that this grace, accepted by faith, is what saves us."[3]

The answer to the faith-versus-works debate is not so difficult to comprehend. The good works we do have inestimable value only because they are done by the grace of Christ and under the inspiration of the Holy Spirit. They are not really the works of the individual, but the works of Christ living within us.

Your works and my works and everybody else's works all put together could never save a single person! Neither could faith alone bring us into the riches of sanctification and holiness. Rather, faith opens the door of God's storerooms, making us "right" with God and able to receive his grace.

When I was a very young priest, I was often assigned to offer Mass at Mount Florence, a training school for delinquent girls run by the Sisters of the Good Shepherd in Peekskill, New

York. It was astonishing to distribute Communion to almost fifty Magdalen Sisters, as they were called. Young and old, black, Anglo, and Hispanic, these women who now led a penitential and contemplative life at one time had been delinquent girls remanded by the courts to the care of the Good Shepherd nuns. When the time came for them to leave, these sisters had opted to remain on as members of the community.

As I was leaving Mount Florence one morning, I saw an elderly Magdalen sister digging a hole in the garden to plant a young sapling. Her venerable face was framed by an old-style habit. I stopped and asked her, "Sister Gertie, how come there are so many Magdalen nuns?" In a strong Polish accent, she responded to me, "Father, when nobody cares what happens to you, God cares what happens to you."

Perhaps Sister Gertie had been like most of the Magdalens, in some kind of difficulty with the law years before. As in the case of most young people who get into such trouble, she may have been neglected or abandoned. But somehow or other— probably through the devoted care of the Sisters of the Good Shepherd—the Lord had communicated to Sister Gertie that he deeply cared about her. Her realization of God's love caused her to change her rebellious ways and embrace a life that was prayerful, penitential, and filled with peace.

Sometimes we have a very clear awareness of our complete dependence on the grace of God. People come up to me and say, "Oh, I listened to your tape. It was wonderful!" I answer, "I had nothing to do with it." I have nothing to do with these words either. I don't even remember writing them. I have to look them over to refresh my memory. I don't have the feeling that these words came from me. I don't feel responsible for them. I don't even live up to them. Sometimes I say things that I never even thought about saying. Sometimes I must admit I don't believe them as completely as I want to. "I believe, Lord; help my unbelief."

Actually, when you listen to me you're really hearing an organ grinder's monkey. You just can't see the organ grinder. So don't gush over my books, sermons, or tapes. Please, pray for me instead. One lovely old Irish lady once wrote me a letter that really put me in my place. She said, "Father, I used to have terrible insomnia. Then I got your tapes. When I listen to them, I go right to sleep." Thank you, God, for not letting me take my works very seriously!

We are all saved by the grace of Christ through faith, not by works lest any person should boast (Eph 2:8-9). To be justified means to be set right with God. Original sin somehow set up an impenetrable wall between God and his children. Humankind became terribly alienated from the Creator when Adam and Eve went over the edge. Jesus Christ came to deliver us. We are saved by Christ alone. Because of his grace, we are brought into the light of his presence.

If you have ever lived a life of sin without uttering a prayer for years, you know what it's like to sit in the shadows. Perhaps you were a believer with some terrible problem you couldn't control, like alcoholism or sexual compulsion. America seems to be crawling with addictions these days, anything from food to sex. You may have been caught. You may have felt powerless against such compulsions, like your life was going down the drain. And then Christ rescued you and set you on a new path. You now have a keen awareness of deliverance or justification.

If you're struggling right now, don't lose heart. In God's redemptive plan, you're sharing in the same drama and suffering our Lord had to endure in order to save the world. You're experiencing your own Calvary, so to speak. Don't give up. Recall what awaited the captain of the guard, a pagan, when he went to Calvary that fateful Friday, expecting to perform once again the gruesome duty of overseeing executions. "Now when the centurion saw what had taken place, he praised God, and said, 'Certainly this man was innocent!'" (Lk 23:47).

FALLING BACK INTO THE DITCH

If you have recently been delivered from a life of habitual sin, I've got news for you: you're going to fall back into sin. The people I'm worried about are Christians who think they never commit sins. I'm very skeptical about "the sinless." The Catholic Church has been putting up with sinners for two thousand years. That's why we Catholics have the Sacrament of Reconciliation or confession.

Our Lord said to the apostles, "I will give you the keys of the kingdom of heaven, and whatever you bind on earth shall be bound in heaven, and whatever you loose on earth shall be loosed in heaven" (Mt 16:19). We invite people to confession as a way of dealing with the ever-present sin in their lives. The saints made use of this precious sacrament very frequently. Pope John Paul II is said to go to confession daily. I know that Mother Teresa goes often. They know they are sinners who live by grace alone. Those who don't recognize or acknowledge their sin don't go to confession. Sadly, the people who need it the most can be the very ones who don't go.

We need to have a clearer sense of deliverance. Suppose you sin or someone you know falls into serious sin. Be consoled by the memory that our Lord Jesus Christ has delivered us all from our sins. Be filled with hope, because the working out of each person's salvation is a long, difficult road.

The apostle Paul may again come to mind as a model of righteousness. He rose to any occasion, no matter what the circumstances. Paul prayed constantly, even in a jail cell after being badly beaten. His faith and hope never seemed to falter. His words of love and encouragement seemed to flow effortlessly in eloquent letters to the churches he had founded. But what did that apparently perfect model say about himself?

I do not understand my own actions. For I do not do what I want, but I do the very thing I hate. Now if I do what I do not want, I agree that the law is good. So then it is no longer I that do it, but sin which dwells within me. For I know that nothing good dwells within me, that is, in my flesh. I can will what is right, but I cannot do it. For I do not do the good I want, but the evil I do not want is what I do.   Rom 7:15-19

I don't know about you, but I can certainly identify with those words. But God wants to give us hope right in the midst of our temptations. The wonderful truth of our justification in Christ should always fill our minds, especially when we are struggling with our sinfulness.

After Paul bitterly laments his own sinful tendencies, he cries out: "Wretched man that I am! Who will deliver me from this body of death? Thanks be to God through Jesus Christ our Lord!" (Rom 7:24-25). Not one to put confidence in his own flesh, Paul drew strength from the source of his deliverance.

A spiritual writer named Fr. Frederick Faber says, "Even in the darkness of mortal sin, faith is constantly preaching." First of all, nobody knows for sure when he or she has committed a mortal sin. Only God knows for sure. A struggling Christian trying to do his or her best and falling through some weakness may not ever be guilty of a mortal sin in the eyes of God. Who knows what *is* in the eyes of God!

A real mortal sin is a terrible reality. Those of you who remember your catechism know that it must be a grave matter, with sufficient reflection, and full consent of the will. This last stricture is a large loophole. According to all the classical moralists, the full consent of the will is impeded by concupiscence— the weakness of the flesh.

Naturally, those who think they have committed a mortal sin should repent as soon as possible. They should be truly sorry and if possible go to confession and receive the Sacrament of Reconciliation. If not possible, they must turn with confidence to Christ in prayer with as pure a heart as they can. But believe me when I tell you about concupiscence! I have heard at least a hundred thousand confessions. And I can't be certain that everything I heard confessed as mortal sins really deserved the label. For sure, the person may be deeply repentant, embarrassed, ashamed, depressed, frustrated, and fed up with him or herself. But did that person have complete freedom of the will when he or she sinned? In many cases, probably not.

Most confessors don't give out serious penances for that very reason. In all of my experience as a confessor, I have given out a serious penance on only one occasion. Don't think that five Our Fathers or Hail Marys, or even a couple of rosaries are a big penance. To say that reciting a rosary is adequate penance for a mortal sin is absurd. I know people who have spent years in serious sin, so ten minutes of prayer can hardly balance the scales.

Only once did I assign a big penance. This fellow really needed to stop the nonsense in his life, so I asked him, "Would you take a serious penance?" When he readily agreed, I told him, "Well, in our monastery there is a very holy brother who loves to go up to the shrine of Our Lady. Would you drive him up?" This was a very saintly brother, very old.

The man replied, "Father, that would not be a penance, that would be an honor." Little did he know.

On a hot Sunday morning in July about half past six, I went out and gave them the blessing. Off they went to the shrine of Our Lady. For four hours, all the way up, they said the rosary, interspersed with psalms, hymns, and canticles. They arrived just in time for the solemn, pontifical Mass under a blazing sun. The liturgy was followed by a "living rosary" in the middle of the baseball field. Little Franco-American girls were dressed up as rosary beads. Still in the blazing sun, this devout brother then enjoyed numerous lively conversations with several very aged nuns about the latest news from Fatima or Garabandal. Finally, four hours back, with—you guessed it—more prayers.

When they got nearer home, the Sunday traffic was backed up, as usual, half-way to Hartford, Connecticut. As they slowly inched their way around Hawthorne Circle, Brother had a little surprise for my penitent: The Seven Dolour Beads, forty-nine Hail Marys in honor of the Seven Sorrows of Our Lady.

I ran into my penitent a few weeks later and asked him about his trip. He said, "It was nice. We said a lot of prayers." I knowingly assured him, "It was a *penance!*" He cracked a wry smile. "You're telling me."

"Well, did it work?" I wanted to know. He answered, "I'm so chaste right now, I feel like I drank Sani-Flush."

That was a great penance, and I haven't given out another

one in twenty-five years. But if you feel you need one, come see me and I will try to arrange something. That dear brother is long dead, but I'm sure we could find somebody else.

FALLING BACKWARDS

We need to remember that justification does not get us onto the road to heaven without the possibility of failure. We can, as St. Paul points out, fall back. He says, "I do not box as one beating the air; but I pommel my body and subdue it, lest after preaching to others I myself should be disqualified (1 Cor 9:26-27). We are warned many times throughout the New Testament to be on guard lest we lose the kingdom. This warning about the Last Judgment is the message of most of the parables of Jesus.

Yet our Lord is constantly calling us back to salvation, for "neither death, nor life, nor angels, nor principalities, nor things present, nor things to come, nor powers, nor height, nor depth, nor anything else in all creation, will be able to separate us from the love of God in Christ Jesus our Lord" (Rom 8:38-39).

Simon Peter denied Jesus three times, and was later given the opportunity to repent when the risen Lord asked him three times, "Do you love me?" (see Jn 21:15-19). We have, on the other hand, the horrifying example of Judas who betrayed the Master but could not bring himself to ask for forgiveness. Both of these disciples committed terrible sins against Jesus. But Peter went on to become the head of the church, while Judas took his own life in utter despair.

No one remains very long in that initial moment of being justified by faith. Once a person is called by Christ, he or she soon jumps up and goes into Damascus like St. Paul, looking for further instructions. St. Bonaventure writes about the person who, once justified and saved, commits sin:

When one has fallen down, he must lie there unless someone lend a helping hand for him to rise. So our soul could not rise completely from these things of sense to see itself and the Eternal Truth in itself unless Truth, assuming human nature in Christ, had become a ladder, restoring the first ladder that had been broken in Adam.

Therefore, no matter how enlightened one may be by the light of natural and acquired knowledge, he cannot enter into himself to delight within himself in the Lord unless Christ be his mediator, who says: "I am the door. If anyone enters through me, he will be saved; and he will go in and out and will find pastures."

We do not draw near to this door unless we believe in him, hope in him and love him. Therefore, if we wish to enter again into the enjoyment of Truth as into paradise, we must enter through faith in, hope in and love of Jesus Christ, the mediator between God and men, who is like the tree of life in the middle of paradise.[4]

"IF CHRIST HAS NOT BEEN RAISED"

The ladder to God was demolished for all by original sin. That ladder is restored by Jesus Christ. We should always acknowledge that Christ alone is our Savior. This clear truth needs to be constantly reiterated in contemporary Christianity. Yet many Americans attend churches of various denominations—all with crosses on the windows and doors—and week after week, month after month, never hear a sermon about how Christ saved the world. Instead, they are fed a lot of pablum. If they feel guilty, their psychotherapists help them work through their feelings.

The marvelous truth of our salvation is that the grace of our Lord Jesus Christ is extended to everyone. Through the providence and mercy of God, Christ can bring deliverance to others in ways that we do not understand or comprehend, outside of the ordinary means of salvation, which is Baptism.

If God's providence uses another way, this does not mean

that anyone is saved without Jesus Christ. If non-Christians are saved, they receive this precious gift the very same way—by the Precious Blood of the only begotten Son of God. They just may not know it. They may have been deprived of that knowledge through no fault of their own.

Most of us have said at some time of a non-believer, "They act more like a Christian than I do." I had a dear friend, a rabbi, who had a great respect and reverence for Christ. Every Christmas he would send me a letter wishing me the best for the Holy Day. Yet he faced persecution as part of a people who were nearly exterminated by the Nazis, members of the then supposedly Christian nation of Germany.

One Easter, this rabbi surprisingly accompanied me to a Protestant sunrise service at the Children's Village where I was the chaplain. When a visiting minister proclaimed in his sermon that Christ did not physically rise from the dead, my rabbi friend whispered, "I should have stayed home in bed. It wouldn't have been a total loss." This man did not believe in Christ's resurrection, but he rightly expected *Christians* to believe in it. He was repeating what another great rabbi, St. Paul, meant when he said, "If Christ has not been raised, then our preaching is in vain and your faith is in vain" (1 Cor 15:14).

We must positively acknowledge every day, every hour, that there is no other way that we are saved except by our Lord Jesus Christ. Would this change our view of things? Absolutely. I could be very worried about many people I know except that I don't have to worry about them. That's the Lord's job. Jesus is the Good Shepherd who leaves the ninety-nine sheep in the wilderness and goes after the one who is lost until he finds it (Lk 15:4). (To bring this point down to a very human level, I will later close this chapter with the personal story of one such strayed soul.)

Would any one of us have any hope of salvation apart from our Lord Jesus Christ? No. No one goes without redemption. No saint stands apart from the salvation of God. Even Our Lady, who was conceived without sin, nevertheless had to be redeemed. The Catholic Church teaches that this redemption took place simultaneously with her conception.

All need to be rescued. That fact should give us immense hope and an immense gratitude to God. Even those who have led a devout life for many years need to be reminded that we all walk on a slippery slope.

The church teaches that the grace of final perseverance cannot be merited. Until the moment we draw our last breath, we are completely dependent on the mercy of God for our salvation. Thank God we are. If I had to live for one moment thinking I was carrying my salvation in my own hands, I'd be frightened to death.

We are in the safest possible place—in the hands of divine mercy. How much we should love Jesus Christ! How much we should honor him, respect him, value him, worship him, adore him!

IN THE HANDS OF DIVINE MERCY

I have a story to tell you about someone who was in the hands of divine mercy, a story of deliverance. Many years ago, my brother, Mark, was stricken by a severe case of childhood diabetes. He was only eleven years old. My uncle, who was a physician, tried to reassure us. He said if my brother just took good care of his health, followed his diet, and took his medication properly, he could lead a normal life—very big "ifs" for a young boy.

As time went on, Mark proved unable to follow those strict rules. Full of bravado, he would never admit to his friends that he had this illness. He took his medicine, of course, or he would have died. But like many people afflicted with diabetes, Mark did not take seriously the dietary requirements and take care of himself. My brother spent his life proving how tough he was—like being a volunteer fire fighter out on a hook-and-ladder truck in the middle of the night.

I knew that Mark had drifted far away from God. I didn't know how far; he was kind enough not to tell me. But I later learned he thought all religion was garbage. I have a picture of him as a teenager at my first Mass. In it, he looks distressed, full of turmoil. As a little boy he had a charming and delightful way about him. We all liked Mark the most because he was always laughing and fooling around.

But after he became ill, Mark began to wrestle with God, like Jacob wrestled with the angel. He fought for many years with God. After he ceased to believe, Mark substituted for God the person who cared for him the most in this world—our human father, Ed. He argued bitterly for years with my dad, whose favorite he was. As it turned out, Mark lived with Dad later on, a man whose greatest desire was to be reunited with his beloved wife in eternity. For the last decade of his life, only one question preoccupied my father: "Will I find Marge on the other side?"

By the providence of God, my brother was alone with my father when he died. My other brothers and sisters had stepped out of the hospital room for a few moments. I was in Ireland giving retreats. When I arrived home for the funeral, Mark met me at the airport with these strange words, "He found her."

"What do you mean?" I asked.

Mark explained, "I was there. I saw the look on his face. He smiled. He found her on the other side." My father had been utterly unresponsive for a month. He had never moved at all during this time. Being a psychologist, the only way I could describe what Mark had seen was as a religious experience. But it was a very powerful experience, the only one my brother had ever had.

Soon this very intelligent, very critical, very worldly-wise and hard-nosed young man joined a prayer group. Not only did he join, Mark became actively involved in the charismatic renewal. His complete turnaround left his relatives and friends mystified. Their reactions ranged from consternation to relief. My sister said, "It's like water turned to wine."

A few months later, I went to see my brother in the hospital.

He was very ill with pneumonia. "How are you doing?" I wanted to know. He said, "I'm dying." I asked, "Are you frightened?" Mark answered, "A little bit, so pray with me." So we prayed together, he in the charismatic way, and we were both comforted.

After I left the hospital room, I discovered I'd forgotten my hat. When I returned to retrieve it, my brother's back was to the door, but I could hear him praying out loud, "Thank you, Jesus. Thank you, Jesus."

Those were the last words I heard Mark say. That night he slipped into a coma. On my father's birthday, my brother was buried.

It was an interesting funeral—a work of the Holy Spirit. Did you know the Holy Spirit has a great sense of humor? The Holy Spirit is always doing things that nobody else would ever dream up—God in his outrageous mode. Mark's funeral was full of the Holy Spirit—a first-class miracle of a funeral.

Standing at the pulpit to say a few words, I realized I had never addressed a more diverse congregation. There sat Mark's old drinking buddies, looking very puzzled. Next to them were sixty members of the prayer group, some place out in spiritual orbit. Next to them sat the uniformed fire department, showing various degrees of consternation, as if they had just come back from a three-alarm fire. Since the Dominican Sisters' infirmary is in our town, I also spotted the retired nuns, including the mother general, who had taught us in school. Next to them sat the Democrats and Republicans who had scrapped with Mark in local politics.

Also in the congregration were grammar school classmates of Mark's children, Mark's divorced wife, and her family. There were the people from the office and an assortment of young women who had been my brother's business colleagues. They looked the most distressed. Apparently after his divorce, Mark had been rather active socially. The congregation also included about twenty-five friars and an assortment of priests, brothers, and sisters.

I looked out at all of them and mused: The only one you can

blame for this is the Holy Spirit. Only he could have pulled this off. Here was the funeral of a thirty-eight-year-old man, struck down partly because he didn't follow the doctor's orders over the years. Mark had grown old very rapidly. Every glass of beer probably cost him a day of his life. He had once thought that religion was garbage; he once hadn't believed in God. How had that happened? And how could his last words have been, "Thank you, Jesus"? An utter mystery.

Mark had been tenderly carried in the hands of divine mercy, just like the young woman I mentioned earlier who died of AIDS. Don't ever give up on anyone you know—no matter how far from God they seem to be. No one can hide beyond the reach of God.

Don't give up on our world. It should have been destroyed long ago, whether by volcanic eruptions or earthquakes or floods or atomic bombs. God is carrying it tenderly in his hands of divine mercy to give more and more people the opportunity to repent.

And don't give up on the church. It would have sunk into oblivion even in the first century if it had stood on its own. It would never have made it even beyond Good Friday, the day all the apostles, save one, deserted the Master. Yet God sends his Holy Spirit over the dark waters and makes all things new. He teaches those who refuse to be taught. He calls to those who refuse to listen. He sometimes uses severe remedies to help people escape from false gods. In his humility, God is willing even to struggle with those who are foolish enough to wrestle with him.

We are all in the hands of divine mercy. God calls to us in the first hour, the third hour, the sixth hour, the ninth hour, and the eleventh hour, the fifty-ninth minute and fifty-ninth second of our lives. If there is someone you know who has strayed from God, keep praying. I prayed for my brother for twenty-seven years. Nothing happened at all—at least that I could see. Even so, you could do a lot worse things with your time than pray for twenty-seven years.

One of the volunteer firemen at Mark's funeral had graduated with me from grammar school. He came up to me in his uniform after the funeral and said, "Sometime when you have five or six hours, stop by the firehouse and explain to me how your brother ever got back to the church."

I could never explain this miracle in five or six *years*, much less five or six *hours*. But I could explain it in one simple sentence: *Jesus delivered my brother.* You and I cannot be saved without him; the whole world cannot be saved without him. But with him, not only we ourselves but also those who are dear to us, those who are far away from God, those who are even his bitterest enemies, may be saved.

If you have been touched by the grace of God early in your life, be grateful. But pray continuously for the gifts of the Holy Spirit, especially the gift of wisdom, that all those in deep spiritual need may have eyes to see and hearts to respond to God's mercy and grace. Everyone needs the hope of deliverance.

Jesus Christ calls us from death to life—precisely what it means to be justified. No matter how difficult our circumstances may be, God calls us to live as a new creation. Even if we are dying from a terminal illness such as cancer or AIDS, we can rejoice that our Lord Jesus Christ has justified us. Mark could die in peace at the age of thirty-eight because he knew Jesus Christ was right there by his side. And I could celebrate my brother's passing from death to life, hoping that one day I would be reunited with him and our parents in that unthinkably beautiful reality we call heaven.

Pray these words with me, a prayer about our deliverance which I have drawn from the one which concludes the fourth book of the *Confessions of St. Augustine:*

◆ ◆ ◆

O Lord Our God, let us trust and hope in the protecting shadow of your wings. Guard us and bear us up. Bear us up, as tiny infants and into our old age. For when you are our strength, we have strength indeed. But when we rely on our-

selves, we only have weakness. When you are with us, our attempts at goodness do not fail. When we turn away from you, we become twisted.

Let us now return to you, O Lord Jesus Christ, that we may not be overcome. For with you we find a perfect goodness which is your presence itself. We have no fear that there is no one to return to merely because we have fallen away from you. Our failures do not cause our hope of eternal life to dim, for you yourself are that everlasting home in which we hope to live with you forever. Amen.

THREE

Help My Unbelief

And Jesus said to him, "If you can! All things are possible to him who believes." Immediately the father of the child cried out and said, "I believe; help my unbelief!"

Mk 9:23-24

A FRIEND OF MINE who is both a dedicated priest and a great character, Fr. Charles McTague, got up the courage to try to visit Albert Einstein at 118 Mercer Street in Princeton, New Jersey. It was shortly after his ordination when this young man arrived unannounced in a black suit and clerical collar. The secretary looked up in surprise. "Yes?"

Charlie bravely asked, "Can I see Dr. Einstein?"

"Do you have an appointment?" When he answered no, the secretary replied, "Then I'm sorry, I don't think you can."

Charlie said, "Well, please ask him."

The secretary seemed a bit put off, but buzzed Dr. Einstein. "There is a Catholic priest down here who wants to see you."

Einstein surprised her. "Send him right up!"

It was as if the world's greatest living scientist had just been waiting for Charlie to arrive. Fr. McTague recalls that Einstein was "the essence of hospitality and humility," a kindly man who made certain his visitor had the most comfortable chair. What was on his mind? Einstein wanted to talk about the Catholic doctrine of the Holy Eucharist and the Mass. He was fascinated by the idea of a substance that could not be seen at all, one that has no color, no shape, and no size! A substance with no accidents, as we say in theology. After about half an hour, Einstein asked Charlie, "Please send me any books in German that you can find that tell me about the Holy Eucharist." And so Charlie did.

Einstein's open-mindedness is by no means universal. As a whole, America is a very materialistic nation. Almost everything we see or hear concerns this natural world. What we call *science* is the study of the material world—the world open to the knowledge of our senses. Because of their training, many people involved in the sciences become incapable of dealing with anything that cannot be detected by the senses. They may even deny the existence of anything which goes beyond the senses. It is well known that Einstein had great respect for religion—even going so far as to observe that while religion without science was blind, science without religion was lame. Even though this brilliant intellectual did not direct his scientific pursuits toward that which is beyond the senses—literally the supernatural—Einstein evidently did not find it hard to accept the possibility of its existence. In fact, he seemed delighted to probe such a wondrous possibility. Unfortunately, most of us get bogged down in one or the other view of reality, the scientific or the spiritual.

NATURE AND BEYOND

Often it is religious people who are accused of being close-minded to the discoveries or theories of science, though people who work in the sciences can be just as narrow-minded. There are many tragic examples of how the pursuit of medical advances has been impeded by such narrow-mindedness. Toward the end of the nineteenth century, the scope of scientific study was strictly limited to what people could see, hear, touch, taste, and smell. Then scientists like Louis Pasteur became aware of creatures invisible to the naked eye. They began to sound the alarm that such microorganisms were causing people to die from infections, especially after surgery.

Do you know that those who made such discoveries were largely held in contempt? The fact that Pasteur was a devout Catholic may have added to the widespread prejudice against his theories. Doctors who accepted this new way of thinking were often regarded as superstitious or crazy. How could there be things people do not see? Surgeons caught washing their hands with an antiseptic before surgery were actually refused courtesy at hospitals or discharged from the staff!

As microscopes were developed, empirical evidence finally confirmed the existence of these organisms. Can you imagine how those doctors felt who persisted in doing surgery without proper preparations? Today they would certainly face an avalanche of lawsuits due to wrongful death! Whoever said that what we don't know or can't see won't hurt us?

A similar phenomenon happened with rays. Wireless radios came into existence because of the discovery of short waves. While playing around in his home, a young man named Marconi found that he was able to send a signal from one pie plate to another across the room without a wire. He eventually used this invisible linkage to send signals from city to city, and finally across the ocean. If you visit Cape Cod, you can still see the foundations of the great towers where Marconi sent wireless signals across the Atlantic Ocean.

Nobody quite understood how Marconi did it. These short-wave radio signals were invisible! Even though we have never *seen* an ultraviolet ray or a gamma ray or an x-ray, they are constantly used in a wide variety of ways. Yet, because the supernatural is not directly available to our senses, its existence is often suspect.

You might say, "There's nothing wrong with that. Science is *supposed* to be limited to the natural or material world." But what do you mean by the material world?

"Well, everybody knows what the material world is." Really? *No one even knows what matter is.* Probably the most popular theory is that the ultimate particle of matter has neither length nor width. It is an indivisible, invisible point of force or energy that doesn't inhere in anything. Clap your two hands together. They appear to be one solid object striking another. But according to this common theory, your hands are not what they appear, but incredibly complex arrangements of points of energy.

Let's consider another example. When I drop my glasses, what tremendous force pulls them down to the floor? You say, "Well, that's gravity." So what is gravity? Are there chains? Invisible threads? Why? How does it work?

Matter and gravity are seemingly simple concepts we take for granted every day. But matter may not be matter. Scientists can't explain exactly how electricity or gravity works. One of the greatest mysteries of all may be how life itself comes into existence. Since nobody quite knows what life is, life is usually defined by its absence. Life is that which is not dead. A recent scientific article on the nature of life stated that if something does not move around and leave little messes after itself, then it's a rock.

We can't get too comfortable with the natural. Nobody seems to know where the natural begins, where it goes, and where it ends. Being initially creatures of nature, we ourselves must approach that which is beyond nature through nature itself. So where does that leave us with the supernatural?

A MYSTERIOUS DOMAIN

So what does all of this have to do with healing the original wound? St. Thomas Aquinas claimed that the greatest obstacle to faith is posed by two problems: the problem of evil and the problem of the supernatural. We have already discussed original sin and its effects on the world in the first chapter. But the supernatural requires us to believe that there is something beyond this world in which we live. Most of us are so caught up in the demands of this life that we rarely stop to ponder what may be beyond it.

Yet our religious faith is founded absolutely on that which goes beyond nature—that which exists in an altogether *separate* domain of being, one that is nonetheless able to influence *this* domain of being in which we human beings make our home. The supernatural occasionally intervenes in our world, even though it is not from, in, or part of the material domain. How does this great mystery happen? No one knows. We can't explain it.

Those who don't accept the reality of the supernatural must have immense problems coming to grips with Jesus Christ. This person came here from another domain of being; then he returned and calls us there to be with him forever. Clergy who get caught up in materialism have an understandable but crippling tendency to water down the reality of faith. The supernatural can seem especially offensive to those who accept all the messages of a culture which simplistically assumes that no such supernatural domain exists. Even worse are those who link its existence with occult or psychic phenomena.

Even many scientists are not well-informed. The most perplexing question in science is, "Where did this reality ultimately come from?" Don't think for a moment that the great scientists ignore that question. It seems obvious to me that the natural world must have come from another domain of being, because there was no material domain of being when this world got started. Where did the universe come from? It came from the world of the supernatural, from the domain of being beyond that which we call nature.

Faith in a personal God and especially in Christ as Son of God, was profoundly rocked when scientists discovered the size of the material universe. When people assumed the earth was the center of the universe, faith in Christ was a bit easier. Learning that the sun was the center of the universe unsettled them. Galileo ran into this problem—which was ultimately that of his critics, not his own. Galileo remained a man of faith. If earth wasn't the center of things, how come the Son of God came *here*? It just didn't add up for some people. The theologians reacted like the physicians who did not accept the existence of microbes.

Then scientists discovered not only our own Milky Way galaxy but also billions of other galaxies filled with hundreds of billions of stars. With all these other worlds in existence, people began to say, "Well, the human race can't be all that special." Yet there is not one shred of scientific evidence that anywhere else in this unbelievably gigantic universe exists one other thinking creature who can say, "Who am I? Where did I come from? Where am I going?"

Perhaps after we have exhausted this age of space exploration, we will come to the strange conclusion that the earth *is* the psychological center of the universe. It will not blow me away if we do discover the existence of other rational creatures in outer space. God is certainly big enough to handle them all. But wouldn't it be funny if at the end of the twenty-first century, all the scientists had to admit, "There ain't nobody else here but us chickens." Wouldn't that be a laugh? They would be in Galileo's situation in reverse. The earth would be the psychological center of the universe. Actually scientists practically have to deal with the earth that way already—because when they measure things in space it is earthly creatures doing the measuring by earthly means.

HIDING FISH SANDWICHES UP YOUR SLEEVES

If you want to believe in the divinity of Christ, you must believe in the world of the supernatural. Otherwise, Christ is either a madman or a liar. Jesus said that he came from the Father, that he had a preincarnate life—a life before he was born into this world. He also spoke of a resurrection life and promised to bring us there to live with him forever. Paul was so impressed with this declaration that he could cry out with the prophet Hosea, "O death, where is thy victory? O death, where is thy sting?" (1 Cor 15:55).

Peter Kreeft refers to the doctrine of Christ's divinity as "the central Christian doctrine, for it is like a skeleton key that opens all the others."[1] Yet both the Jews and Gentiles found it a stumbling block. "That a man who was born out of a woman's womb and died on a cross, a man who got tired and hungry and angry and agitated and wept at his friend's tomb, that this man who got dirt under his fingernails should be God was, quite simply, the most astonishing, incredible, crazy-sounding idea that had ever entered the mind of man in all human history."[2]

To the crowds in the New Testament, Christ was known as "*the one who does miracles.*" People clamored to get close to him, asking, "Lord, that I may see... that I may be clean... that my little boy may not die." Jesus Christ responded to their pleas by working miracles—human actions which suspended the natural laws of science. The eminent Catholic scholar of Scripture, Rudolph Schnackenberg, maintains that Jesus demanded faith of all who met him, even pagans—that they believe he could help them by working signs that went beyond the powers of nature. He did these signs directly by the power of God.[3]

Many people pussyfoot around these supernatural works of Christ. They say that he didn't really perform miracles. Some theorize that everybody came to the multiplication of the loaves and fishes with fish sandwiches hidden in their sleeves and then brought them out when Jesus gave the order! I have actually read that. Please! Just tell me you're an atheist. Tell me you don't believe in Christianity. I can deal with that. But don't tell me something so far-fetched.

The great apologist Frank Sheed once told me that when some scholars cut the miracles out of the New Testament, all they leave you with is a handful of confetti. Pope John Paul II has given an extensive teaching on the miracles of Jesus. He identifies the reason why some scholars deny the historical validity of such accounts as a rationalist prejudice against the supernatural.[4]

In brief, the widely accepted ideas of the Enlightenment in the eighteenth century were opposed to the notion of any direct divine intervention in history after creation. Many thought such interventions impossible, others considered them unlikely. While dismissing many tales and legends of the preternatural or even of the falsely identified supernatural, the proponents of the Enlightenment dismissed the miracles of Jesus as well. The foundation of such a position is deism, the idea that God creates but is unconcerned about the finite world. He's more like a clockmaker who sets everything into motion (creation) and then views it from afar—instead of a personal God who is about a work of redemption and sanctification in the human heart. The pope suggests that some scholars have denied the supernatural in their attempts to preserve the credibility of Christianity for those made sceptical by an uncritical acceptance of such principles of the Enlightenment.

But what does the Catholic Church teach about Christ? In a nutshell, that he is the only begotten Son of God; that he preexisted; that he came out of eternity; that he survived death; that as the Son of God, he is equal to the Father.

Those who denied this truth in the past were called Arians or worse; those who deny it today are often labeled modernists, so don't let anyone mislead you. We even recite this truth every Sunday just so we won't forget: Christ is *God from God, light from light, true God from true God, begotten not made, one in being with the Father, through whom all things were made.* If that's not clear, then nothing is clear.

Jesus also was the Son of Man, a child of the human race. The Catholic Church throughout its history has defended his humanity. He walked, talked, got angry, grew tired, and became annoyed with people. As a human being, Jesus was subject to dying and, in fact, was murdered.

In keeping with the New Testament, the church teaches that Christ came to bring us eternal salvation by our adoption through him as children of God. Jesus did this by obedience—taking on our miserable, fallen human condition. Jesus Christ came to earth as a mere baby. The church celebrates his incarnation in the beautiful feast of Christmas.

Knowing our powerlessness to overcome sin and death, God sent his Son, innocent of sin, to pay the price for us. Jesus was willing to obey his Father, no matter what the cost, in order to see us restored. Blessed Julian writes:

> I set my eyes on the same cross that had comforted me before. I set my tongue to speak of Christ's Passion and to recite the creed. I set my heart on God with all my trust and with all my might.
>
> It is God's will that I should see myself as bound to him in love as if all that he has done he has done for me alone. And so should every soul think inwardly of its lover.
>
> He wills that our hearts should be lifted high above the depths of earthly and vain sorrows, and rejoice in him. He loves us and enjoys us, and so he wills that we love him and enjoy him, and firmly trust him; and all shall be well.[5]

Beyond the cross, we are also saved by Christ's victory over death, by his resurrection from the dead. Paul stressed this in his first letter to the Corinthians: "Now if Christ is preached as raised from the dead, how can some of you say that there is no resurrection of the dead? But if there is no resurrection of the dead, then Christ has not been raised; if Christ has not been raised... your faith is futile and you are still in your sins" (1 Cor 15:12-17).

Finally we are saved by his second coming—by his bodily return to earth. A rabbi and a priest were once having an argument about the difference between Christianity and Judaism. The rabbi said, "I believe the Messiah is coming and you believe the Messiah is coming again!" That sums it up very well, indeed.

Christ revealed something intensely interesting about God which no one really knew before. Ancient Judaism had hinted at it in obscure ways. When the Jews of that time referred to God, they used terms like the Almighty, Adonai, the Holy One, the Unnameable One. But they also spoke about the Spirit of

God which would come into a prophet. Was this spirit the same as or less than God? Or perhaps an angel? No one knew.

When our Lord Jesus Christ came, he revealed the *Trinity:* the Father, the Son, and the love between them which becomes a third person—the Holy Spirit. Out of all eternity, before anything else came into being, this relationship existed. The divine being did not spend eternity alone, so to speak. Although there was one God, there was within that one being a mysterious relationship, a tangible bond of love.

Christ revealed not only the existence of this relationship of love but the incredible fact that it was freely shared with creatures—especially with the human creature, this unique thinking being, possibly like nothing else in the whole material universe.

We know there is a thinking creature in another domain called an angel. Most of us are very fuzzy about angels, usually pictured as physically attractive youths with blond hair, blue eyes, and wings. Have you ever seen a picture of an ugly angel? Actually, much of this symbolism stands as an obstacle to thinking seriously about the beings referred to by St. Augustine as "celestial citizens." Angels, literally "messengers of God," are frequently mentioned in Scripture. They carry out important tasks in the Gospels—like the Angel of the Annunciation or the Angel of Agony.

Angels possess a certain purity and simplicity—no complex moving parts, so to speak—and lack the weakness of the flesh. Consequently, they made only one important and irreversible decision: to obey God or to join the rebellion spearheaded by Lucifer the Archangel. The Christian faith includes a belief in the existence of fallen angels, and the immense harm that they have done to human beings, who are one step below them in the order of being.

Angels can say yes and no to God. Human beings can say yes, no, maybe, contradict themselves, repent, go back on their repentance, commit ten thousand sins, and still die as saints! This peculiar human creature was loved by God so much that the Son of God came into the world to save it. "For God so loved the world that he gave his only Son, that whoever believes in him should not perish but have eternal life" (Jn 3:16).

St. Catherine of Siena lived through the same troubled times as Julian of Norwich. Thus their prayers have much in common. The following is entitled "The Bonds of Love." It magnificently portrays the tangible love of God made human, made flesh. The Son who was worshiped by angels came and sought the response of love from the human creature.

My Lord, turn the eye of your mercy on your people and on your mystic body, holy Church. How much greater would be your glory if you would pardon so many and give them the light of knowledge! For then they would surely all praise you, when they see that your infinite goodness has saved them from deadly sin and eternal damnation. How much greater this than to have praise only from my wretched self, who have sinned so much and am the cause and instrument of every evil! So I beg you, divine eternal Love, to take your revenge on me, and be merciful to your people. I will not leave your presence till I see that you have been merciful to them.

For what would it mean to me to have eternal life if death were the lot of your people, or if my faults especially and those of your other creatures should bring darkness upon your bride, who is light itself? It is my will, then, and I beg it as a favor, that you have mercy on your people with the same eternal love that led you to create us in your image and likeness. You said, "Let us make humankind in our image and likeness." And this you did, eternal Trinity, willing that we should share all that you are, high eternal Trinity! You, eternal Father, gave us memory to hold your gifts and share your power. You gave us understanding so that, seeing your goodness, we might share the wisdom of your only-begotten Son. And you gave us free will to love what our understanding sees and knows of your truth, and so share the mercy of your Holy Spirit.

Why did you so dignify us? With unimaginable love you looked upon your creatures within your very self, and you fell in love with us. So it was love that made you create us and give us being just so that we might taste your supreme eternal good. Then I see how by our sin we lost the dignity you had given us.

Rebels that we were, we declared war on your mercy and became your enemies. But stirred by the same fire that made you create us, you decided to give this warring human race a way to reconciliation, bringing great peace out of our war. So you gave us your only-begotten Son, your Word, to be mediator between us and you. He became our justice taking on himself the punishment for our injustices. He offered you the obedience you required of him in clothing him with our humanity, eternal Father, taking on our likeness and our human nature!

O depth of love! What heart could keep from breaking at the sight of your greatness descending to the lowliness of our humanity? We are your image, and now by making yourself one with us you have become our image, veiling your eternal divinity in the wretched cloud and dung heap of Adam. And why? For love! You, God, became human and we have been made divine! In the name of this unspeakable love, then, I beg you—I would force you even!—to have mercy on your creatures.[6]

CALVARY IN THE BRONX

Many fine books going back to the Fathers of the Church have explored the great truths of salvation. I encourage you to read some of them. My purpose here is not to teach the great mystery of Christ but to help you to live it in your own life. Christ rose from the dead and dwells among us, still able in some mysterious way to touch the believer in all the circumstances of this existence. Jesus said, "Lo, I am with you always, to the close of the age" (Mt 28:20).

Many have seen his glory in the sunrise and in the sunset. But then you can also see Christ in a neighborhood that is poor and ugly. To find Christ at all times, you must be able to recognize him in what can only be called repulsive.

When we began our new religious communities of reform in 1987, we were very aware of two things: that we wanted to be loyal to the spirit of St. Francis, and that we were in a very precarious situation. One serious mistake and our little endeavor could have been destroyed. Therefore we opened the first friary of our new community in a rough section of the South Bronx, referred to as Fort Apache—not because the place is populated by native Americans, but because being on duty there as a police officer seemed reminiscent of the early frontier. Sometimes I think the leaders of the Apache tribe ought to sue New Yorkers for using this designation.

Fort Apache in the Bronx boasts the lowest per capita income of any congressional district. Blocks of ruined buildings and even more blocks of vacant lots are filled with garbage and debris. Amid the violence and widespread disease (especially tuberculosis and AIDS), live thousands of poor mothers, fathers, and children, working hard to eke out a hand-to-mouth existence or else just admitting defeat and giving up. For a community that wanted to live the poverty of St. Francis, it seemed the best place we could find.

While it will be difficult for most readers to imagine what this corner of the world is like, working there offers profound spiritual lessons. We became convinced that not only can Christ's presence be found in such a place, but it can be even more obvious, more inescapable, in just such a place. Christ himself tells us, in the description of the Last Judgment, that he is to be found among the poor, sick, hungry, homeless, and imprisoned (see Mt 25).

I myself have been helping homeless people since the age of nineteen, when I was in charge of the "poor lads" who came to the monastery to eat. I can tell you that Christ is there to be seen by those who have eyes to see him. He is there in disguise—just as he was when he walked along the dusty roads and healed the leprous beggars. The voice of God is to be heard in the slums—just as it was by the large, hillside crowds that had to strain to hear his words at the Sermon on the Mount. His divinity is hidden in most of the events of life.

The divinity of our Lord Jesus Christ was also hidden on the cross at Calvary, where his battered body was stripped naked and pounded with nails. His flesh was ripped and his blood flowed for us. The chief priest and elders mocked him, saying, "He saved others; he cannot save himself. He is the King of Israel; let him come down now from the cross, and we will believe in him" (Mt 27:42). Jesus cried out in agony for his Father's embrace: "My God, my God, why hast thou forsaken me?" But he endured and yielded up his spirit to his Father. To find the real Christ, you must be able to find him at Calvary.

A WONDERFUL GIFT

We have a wonderful gift to keep us aware of the presence of Christ in our lives in the Sacrament of the Body and Blood of Christ. Although Christ is everywhere, the Holy Eucharist focuses our attention on his very real presence in our world. In the Blessed Sacrament, both Christ's divinity and humanity are hidden. We believe that Christ is fully divine and fully human; Christ is in heaven and on earth. He is where we are going and he is with us now.

As we have seen, even Einstein sensed something of this mystery. How much we Catholics should treasure the Holy Eucharist as the very center of our lives! Yet I often notice people entering the church who don't genuflect or who just give a little nod toward the tabernacle. I'm not impressed.

Therefore, one of our first decisions as a reformed community was to spend at least an hour every day in adoration of Christ hidden in the Blessed Sacrament. We desperately needed Christ with us and he was there for the finding. Once I saw a Protestant monk, Brother Roger of Taizé, kneel down and put his face against the floor before the giant tabernacle in his Church of the Reconciliation. After a long period of prayer, he turned to me and said, "The real presence of Jesus Christ in the world, the Blessed Sacrament of the Catholic Church." And Brother Roger was a Calvinist!

St. Peter Julian Eymard wrote, "Give me the Eucharist, or let me die!" Just a pious exaggeration? No! Without the ongoing nourishing presence of the Eucharist I think my life would be without hope spiritually or morally. I would be lost for certain. Salvation comes through faith in Christ, who is present in every tabernacle where the Blessed Sacrament is reserved.

Paradoxically, finding Christ in the Eucharist helps me to find him everywhere else. Francis Thompson, the great mystical poet of the English language, wrote "The Orient Ode" in which he sees day like a priest bringing the monstrance, the flaming sun through the sky, to the evening benediction. The end of the poem reads:

> By this, O Singer, know we if thou see.
> When men shall say to thee: Lo! Christ is here,
> When men shall say to thee: Lo! Christ is there,
> Believe them: yea, and this—then art thou seer,
> When all thy crying clear
> Is but: Lo here! lo there!—ah me, lo, everywhere![7]

Poets often say it the best. The great Irish poet and editor of *The Irish Times*, Joseph Plunkett, was executed by the British government in 1916 in Mountjoy prison in Dublin for signing the Irish Declaration of Independence. He wrote the following words, which we have framed and hung on the wall of the Trinity Retreat House:

> I see His blood upon the rose
> And in the stars the glory of His eyes,
> His body gleams amid eternal snows,
> His tears fall from the skies.
>
> I see His face in every flower;
> The thunder and the singing of the birds

Are but His voice—and carven by His power
Rocks are His written words.

All pathways by His feet are worn,
His strong heart stirs the ever-beating sea,
His crown of thorns is wound with every thorn,
His cross is every tree.[8]

THE COSMIC CHRIST

Let's consider another aspect of Christ as our Savior: the "Cosmic Christ." As more and more people are affected by the New Age Movement, we need to clarify this term which is so freely bandied about. People who are trying to make some kind of link between the New Age and Christian thinking propose that the Cosmic Christ is a pre-Christian archetype of the God-consciousness in every creature, the divine "I AM" in every person, a sort of divine pattern. According to this view, Jesus is one incarnation of the Cosmic Christ, perhaps the most powerful, but everyone is called to give birth to this reality within themselves and society.

Matthew Fox, a well-known proponent of the so-called Cosmic Christ concept, proclaims that everyone will know themselves to be "divine and human, animal and demon. We are Cosmic Christs."[9] Such New Age theology strikes me—among other things—as a failure to recognize our Lord as the only begotten Son of God.

There is a reality referred to as the "Cosmic Christ." Not only does Christ dwell with us in the Holy Eucharist, not only is he present where two or three are gathered in his name, not only is he present among the poor and the weak and the lonely. But if you were an astronaut on the moon, you could cry out to Christ and he would be there, because he is the eternal Word of God through whom all things are created.

As the Gospel of St. John says so strikingly, "All things were made through him, and without him was not anything made that was made" (Jn 1:3). He is saying that Christ is everywhere. But you have to be very careful that you don't misunderstand his presence as something like a world soul. Belief in a kind of cosmic presence has always pervaded paganism and natural religions. Ancient people often believed in a "world soul," as if creation itself has a soul. That is not Christ. Such a cosmic soul or thinking, living spirit is not a reality.

Buddhism and Hinduism are well-developed religions which include a deep belief in the supernatural. Their "world soul" may reflect an innate need to believe in a cosmic Christ, but such is not the teaching of the Catholic Church. Many are very interested in Eastern spirituality these days, and thank God they're interested in some form of religion. But unfortunately, they sometimes give up Christianity to become involved in beliefs that are fundamentally opposed to true Christian beliefs.

You have to be very careful of some conceptions of Christ as the greatest of the manifestations of the cosmic world soul. The Hindu people believe in avatars—human beings that are so holy, so divine, that they are incarnations of the world soul or of the Divine Being. That's not Christ. Christ is *not* the avatar of avatars. He's not the guru of gurus. Even if the Hindus claimed Christ as the greatest of all the incarnations of the divine, I would not agree just to be religiously tolerant. I would respect this belief, but I could not accept it.

One has to be careful when one speaks of Jesus Christ. What would you think if I said that Christ was a clergyman? You'd be a bit uncomfortable, I suspect. Suppose I said that Christ was a monsignor or a bishop or a pope? Would that be any better? No! We clergy are only representatives. The pope is the Vicar of Christ; he is not Christ. A sister who was the head of the Holy Ghost Hospital in Rome introduced herself to Pope John XXIII by saying, "I'm the superior of the Santo Spiritu." The pope shot back, "The superior of the Holy Ghost! I'm only the Vicar of Christ."

Since Jesus was so insightful when dealing with people, shall we say he's a psychologist? Blasphemy! There are only two occupational titles you can attach to our Lord with a straight face. You can say he was a carpenter. He isn't a carpenter now, but he *was* a carpenter. You can also say that he was a rabbi. But in the New Testament, Jesus is proclaimed to be a priest forever, the Priest of the whole creation as it worships the Godhead. But a psychologist, clergyman, monsignor, bishop, pope, world soul, avatar of avatars, guru of gurus, nicest guy that ever lived? Forget it!

FOLLOWING THE REAL JESUS CHRIST

The real Christ who walked this earth was a blue-collar worker, a carpenter. He lived in the humble country town of Nazareth, which is still a backwater. The entrance to the town looks surprisingly like that of the Bronx—strewn with rusting old cars. When I first saw all those wrecks, I couldn't help thinking, "I never left home!"

Despite the glorious settings of much religious art, we must never forget the *reality*. Our Lord was a very poor man who gave up his carpenter shop to live the life of an itinerant preacher. He lived with the poor and he loved the poor. Regarding the feeding of the five thousand, we read, "As he landed he saw a great throng, and he had compassion on them, because they were like sheep without a shepherd; and he began to teach them many things" (Mk 6:34).

In America, the message is to be rich. There is no day when this media-hype contradiction of Christ is more obvious than Christmas, the celebration of his birth. In a paradoxical and almost blasphemous contradiction of the true meaning of Christmas, many become even more materialistic. The stores are overflowing with goods during the holidays. Some of this stuff is useful—like clothing. Some of it is simply amusing to children, like toys. Some of it is nothing more than junk, stuff we don't need and never will.

As a matter of fact, our friaries are filled at Christmas time with gifts for the poor in a meager attempt to take the edge off their pain, to bring them a little joy. I wish I could go to them and say, "Be glad and rejoice that you are poor." But they wouldn't understand. So we give them a few tangible things in the hope that they will see them as symbols of God's love.

After we deliver food and several gifts to each child on our list—gifts lovingly prepared by generous volunteers from the suburbs—we finally go to the poorest street in New York City, the home of a large number of dispossessed people from Latin America and Africa. There, we empty the van of all that's left. On Christmas Day, a number of poor and needy families come to our retreat house for dinner. I work in the homeless shelter that night.

In the midst of this joyful giving, I have a small celebration of my own. Toward the end of the evening, I pour myself a small paper cup of wine—preferably sherry—and toast myself in the bathroom mirror. I look at the reflection of this old face and say, "Benedict, Merry Christmas!" You can celebrate Christmas any way you like, but that's my way. I have a marvelous time. I really have the feeling that I celebrate it with Jesus. Don't laugh until you try it yourself and see!

DRENCHED IN BLOOD

Those who live by the faith preached by the carpenter of Nazareth—a faith in a loving and forgiving God, a faith calling for charity and justice for all—have been persecuted almost since its very beginning. Faith in Jesus Christ as the Son of God is drenched in blood. Those who practice it are challenged and persecuted at times even by those who claim to be believers.

When our little religious communities of Sisters and Friars of the Renewal were getting started, we thought it would be good to send everyone to Rome. Since the original friars had to visit the Congregation of Religious, we brought the sisters, the postulants, and the novices along as well. I hoped that we could have our picture taken in St. Peter's Square. That photograph of our little group now hangs in my room.

In front of St. Peter's is a gigantic obelisk, carved out of granite by the Egyptians. The Romans brought it back and put it in the center of Nero's circus. Around that stone monument, thousands of people were killed for their faith in Christ. It was literally bathed in the blood of the martyrs, including Agnes, Agatha, and Perpetua. These victims were hacked to pieces by the gladiators, eaten alive by lions and tigers, or burned in the shadow of that obelisk.

After the new basilica had been built, one of the popes had the obelisk moved to the center of St. Peter's Square. A huge cross now sits atop the granite, and on the base is carved in Latin: *"Christ conquers, Christ captains, Christ commands. Christ delivers his people from all evil."*

How does Christ conquer? He conquers by shedding his blood, by the blood of his martyrs. He lives by doing; he wins by losing. Down through the ages Christ has won the battle for salvation by the death of martyrs.

Perhaps some illustrations will help explain such a paradox. Have you ever seen the film *Romero,* about Archbishop Oscar Romero of El Salvador? An exiled Franciscan bishop who served in that country told me that Archbishop Romero was in every way a devout, quiet, gentle priest who was drawn against his inclinations into political controversy because of his objection to cruel government policies. He denounced the piratical abuse of the poor, especially the mass killing of innocent people by the so-called death squads.

Romero depicts a marvelous scene in which Archbishop Romero arrives at a desecrated church which still holds the Blessed Sacrament. A mercenary soldier guards the doors and threatens to kill him if he walks in. While the crowd silently watches, this courageous archbishop walks past the machine guns pointed at him and enters the church.

The camera then focuses on an old woman standing in the crowd—not an actress, but a toothless native from that area with Indian features suggesting nobility of character. This woman follows the archbishop. When everyone else enters after her, the soldiers put down their guns.

High drama indeed, but that's how Christ conquers. "Not by might, nor by power, but by my Spirit, says the LORD of hosts" (Zec 4:6).

We should all be outraged by the atrocities committed in El Salvador and several other Central American countries—especially the murder of six priests in 1989. As university professors they had criticized the governing political party, which the world had already denounced for the assassination of Archbishop Romero while he celebrated the liturgy of the Eucharist. Thirty men killed these six priests in cold blood, along with their innocent housekeeper and her child. Some of them were eventually brought to trial, but many have escaped justice so far. I felt the same outrage at the murder of several American sisters a few years before, including one of my former students at Maryknoll.

Unquestionably, religious titles are sometimes used for political purposes. Right, left, or center, such a stance is often unwise. It is usually far better for the church to remain largely aloof from political alliances. Even those who appear to be heroes have feet of clay. But it is far more important that church leaders break free from their own weakness, so as to preach the gospel to all.

Don't worry about the martyrs. The blood of the martyrs is the seed of the church. It has been said that martyrs begin their most important work the day they die. I'm not worried about the Catholic Church in the countries of Central America. We should protest, but we need not worry. If they have priests, religious, and laity who are willing to risk their lives in the cause of justice, then the beatitude applies to them: "Blessed are those who hunger and thirst for righteousness, for they shall be satisfied.... Blessed are those who are persecuted for righteousness' sake, for theirs is the kingdom of heaven" (Mt 5:6, 10).

Our Lord himself issued a severe warning to those who abuse religion for their own purposes or those who persecute religion because it tells them the truth. St. John the Baptist was killed by a cheap political hack, King Herod, who had married his brother's wife. When John the Baptist denounced this scandal, Herod had John beheaded at the connivance of his wife and stepdaughter.

Let us pray earnestly for the conversion of our enemies, for the conversion of the men who killed the priests and sisters in Central America, for the conversion of political murderers throughout the world. Let us pray especially for those civil leaders who abuse their office to keep themselves in power. They have a curse upon their heads which is as old as the curse of King Herod and the curse of pharaoh.

I wouldn't want to be them; I wouldn't want to even be related to them. I feel sorry for the families who have to live with those murderers. I pray that they will be brought to repentance. But let us also pray for ourselves, that we will not fail to give witness to Jesus Christ in these unbelieving times.

REAL FAITH CALLS FOR REAL COURAGE

You may not see yourself as having any great effect in public life, but you all have neighbors, you work some place, you know people, you have family members who are confused by secular values. We are called to be witnesses to the life and light of Christ. We all can proclaim the glorious truth of salvation. Jesus said, "Every one who acknowledges me before men, I also will acknowledge before my Father who is in heaven; but whoever denies me before men, I also will deny before my Father who is in heaven" (Mt 10:32-33).

It is easy to forget that the faith of Christ may call for inconvenience, misunderstanding, rejection, and even shedding of blood. A wise believer will not lose sight of these possibilities, and may often need to repent for not being a more genuine witness.

I recall a frail little woman in her late fifties, who had few financial resources and a skimpy kind of job. She was telling me quite blandly that she was getting ready to go to jail for six months. She had given up her modest apartment, put her few possessions in storage, and given notice at her job—with no assurance that she would get it back. She later participated in a rescue at an abortion clinic, would not plead guilty, and was sentenced to jail.

While I agreed with her on the iniquity of abortion, I counseled her on some procedures that might protect the little security she possessed. She was way ahead of me. I stopped in the middle of my efforts to realize she understood something I had forgotten. Whether I agreed with her decision or not, she was very clear on one basic fact: that faith in Christ may bring suffering to his disciples.

If you find this lesson too tough to swallow, recall those words carved on that monument to martyrdom in St. Peter's Square: "Christ conquers, Christ captains, Christ commands. Christ delivers his people from all evil." We must not lose hope, and we must not run away.

STORM CLOUDS GATHERING ON THE HORIZON

In cooperating with God's work to bring healing and deliverance to all, the Catholic Church must be constant. For decades, disciples of Christ persevered as they faced persecution, social ostracism, and even death to keep the gospel alive in Eastern Europe and the former Soviet Union. Now we see it springing to life everywhere.

When the Iron Curtain fell, I almost felt sorry for those who were set free from Communist oppression. They were about to be hit with a tidal wave of drugs, pornography, morally destructive videos and entertainment. Which is better: open persecution or a blitz of corruption?

We have been praying for seventy years for the conversion of Russia. We had better start praying for the conversion of America which exports such toxic moral waste. We ought to be concerned about the worldly Babylon in which we live. The question which now looms is, *when will America be converted?*

Archbishop Fulton Sheen once commented that Russia possessed the cross without Christ, but that the United States had Christ without the cross. Neither conforms with God's plan for salvation as revealed in Jesus Christ his only Son. To be true disciples of Christ, we must embrace the cross and be prepared to lay down our lives. Jesus tells his disciples, "If any man would come after me, let him deny himself and take up his cross and follow me. For whoever would save his life will lose it, and whoever loses his life for my sake will find it. For what will it profit a man, if he gains the whole world and forfeits his life?" (Mt 16:24-26).

We live in sad, unbelieving times of individual and institutional hypocrisy—times which flaunt every law of God, including infanticide. Polls today show that people increasingly support helping those who suffer painful and incurable diseases to take their own lives. We've already returned to the time of the Coliseum when the entertainment industry daily brings into our living rooms violent dramatizations of death and murder. Parents whose children are corrupted by that garbage hardly seem to realize the grave impact.

The day is coming when euthanasia will be imposed on the aged, infirm, mentally retarded, and physically handicapped. We're talking about murder! Indeed, the day may already be upon us. Dr. Jack Kevorkian of Michigan, known as Dr. Death, is a vocal proponent of doctor-assisted suicide. He has assisted in the suicides of several people, who wanted to end their prolonged suffering. He simply hooked them up to a simple machine, so they could administer a lethal dose of poison. A charge of murder was lodged against him by the state but later dropped. In Europe, the Netherlands allows doctors to perform euthanasia on the elderly and incurably ill.

A society that judges some unworthy of life will ultimately instill suspicion and terror into families. Some parents will look at their own children and worry, "Someday, will this child sign my death warrant?" The young and healthy will find it easy to say, "Why waste all this money on the care of a mentally ill or senile person when it could be put to better use?"

What is the legitimate use of money and resources if not the care of life? If money is for power and pleasure first, we will become submerged in a diabolically controlled society not unlike the harrowing "Brave New World" described by George Orwell's *1984*. Just who would make decisions about who would be killed? Every one of us may be old and senile someday—God willing.

As such storm clouds gather, it is important to remember: *Christ conquers.* Not by violence, but by love; not by the words of men and women, but by the illumination of the Holy Spirit; not by guns and tanks, but by works of mercy and charity; not by soldiers and armies, but by the humble prayers of devout believers; not by the blood of his enemies, but by the blood of his martyrs.

Christ conquers in only one place—the human heart. That is where the gaping wound of original sin must be healed. As we ponder the mercy and love of God, we need to remember the ghastly reality of sin and evil. The world pretends to think in terms of love and mercy while it avoids thinking about the immorality it condones.

EVIL AND ITS UNDOING

A grave mistake made by many today is denying the evil of sin through nice thoughts about God's compassion and mercy. No one can remain faithfully at the foot of the cross and deny the utterly grotesque reality which killed the Son of God. Jesus endured the agony because of sin to take away sin. Granted, much moral evil is done by a few very corrupt people who think nothing of exterminating countless innocent victims who happen to get in their way. Consider the examples of Hitler and

Stalin, and more recently, Pol Pot of the Khmer Rouge in Cambodia, who annihilated his own people.

But a lot of evil is also done by those who are selfish, ignorant, culpably uninformed, and weak—which includes you and me. Far from thinking that sin is nothing at all, the great mystics say that evil is so awful that we can't bear to look it in the face. Blessed Julian warns us:

> In his mercy our Lord shows us our sin and our weakness by the kindly light of himself. For our sin is so vile and so horrible that he, in his courtesy, will not show it to us except by the light of his grace and his mercy.
>
> He, in his courtesy, limits the amount we see, for it is so vile and so horrible that we could not bear to see it as it is. And so, by humbly knowing our sins through contrition and grace, we shall be broken from all things that are not like our Lord. Then shall our blessed Savior wholly heal us and make us one with him.
>
> The greatest worship we can give to him is penitence, to live gladly and gaily because of his love.[10]

PENITENCE—THE ANTIDOTE TO EVIL

Our blessed Savior can heal those who become penitent. But what is penitence? Penitence is following the poor and truthful Jesus Christ. May we pray that by the grace of the Holy Spirit, he will conquer in our hearts and continue to deliver his people from all evil. May we pray for greater faith, that Christ would help our unbelief. May he give us eyes to see who he really is who dwells in our midst—God with us, God who has come to save.

The poverty and evil in this world must bring us to pray and work for salvation. Unfortunately, we often fall in step with a wretched, miserable, stinking, rotten, diabolical anti-culture, if only by being passive or silent. (Notice I call it anti-culture and not popular culture.) The Christian is called not only to *appreciate* Christ but to *follow* Christ. Have we forgotten that?

You know the problem with us Christians in America? Our Christ is too rich! Not the real Christ, not the eternal Son of God born in a manger, not even the Cosmic Christ—but the Christ of our imagination, our personal image of the Son of God. While Jesus himself was a poor person who daily embraced suffering, many of us spin our wheels trying to avoid suffering. How seriously do we believe in the *poor* Jesus Christ? How willing are we to suffer with him and be humiliated for him?

When I walk from the subway to our friary on 156th Street in the Bronx, I say to myself, "What am I doing in New York? What am I doing in this apocalyptic vision?" I walk past a little graffiti shrine crudely painted on the wall of a demolished building and decorated with a cross, a vigil candle, a can with some flowers. The sign says, "Good-bye, José. Go with God." José was a teenager shot to death on that spot. There are no suspects, no warrants, just the rumor that it had to do with drugs.

If Dante visited the Bronx, he would have added an eighth level to hell in *The Inferno*. Why am I here? Because this is where God wants me—in this city where the powers of darkness and light clash with the greatest intensity. New York City exudes extraordinary contrasts, like cathedrals alongside palaces of sin. I think there may be more people per square inch who go to church every day in New York than almost any other city in the world. Six thousand people a day walk through the doors of St. Patrick's Cathedral alone. Yet the city oozes with the evils of drugs, robbery, prostitution, and murder—not to mention white-collar corruption and crime.

This is where Christ *is* for me. And when he is not here for me, he waits for me in the pulpit or in the confessional. Most of you probably live in places less apocalyptic than the Bronx. Where does Christ wait for you? You need to find him there.

Blessed Julian teaches that we suffer from two kinds of sickness that drag us down in our fight against evil. One is impatience with the pains and troubles which bear down upon us;

the other is despair and fearfulness. These are the evils that most trouble the human soul. God wills to cure us of them.

Our Lord showed us his patience in his gruesome passion, as well as his joy and delight in his passionate love for us. He showed us by his example that we should bear our pains gladly and wisely. When we do so, we give glory to God and find great happiness. We Christians may be anxious that the world come to believe, but we are flawed witnesses unless we suffer bravely and gladly. Let us stir up faith by rejoicing with Christ in pain and suffering!

THE JAWS OF HELL WILL NOT PREVAIL

Our Lord's warning that "The powers of death shall not prevail against [the church]" certainly suggests the forces of darkness are going to try (Mt 16:18). During the centuries since the death of Christ, the jaws of hell have been continuously grinding down upon his body on earth. Hell has attacked the church with scandal, persecution, heresy, confusion, and unbelief. The powers of darkness have, on occasion, reached into its highest corridors, corrupting popes and leading theologians into heresy. No one is immune to deception.

Let me cite an example from my own city: a "Stop the Church" rally in November, 1989, in front of St. Patrick's Cathedral. One day I received a brochure with the picture of Cardinal O'Connor, reading: "We must attack the church for a scandalous teaching on abortion and for its murderous policy on AIDS."

"A scandalous teaching on abortion?" We're going to great ends to keep children alive. A "murderous policy on AIDS"? No single private agency in the city of New York expends more effort on the care of AIDS victims than the Catholic Church. The Terrence Cardinal Cooke Medical Center, a hospital for people who are chronically ill, is gradually being transformed

into one of the leading medical centers for research and treatment of AIDS in the world.

The organization that announced this rally is called ACT-UP (Aids Coalition to Unleash Power), a direct-action political group trying to persuade the government to treat AIDS and health care as a political issue. Its intention for this particular rally was to "stop the church" by disturbing a Sunday liturgy. ACT-UP was joined by several militant pro-abortion groups. I find it interesting that we Catholics are not the only church in New York, but we were identified as "the church" to be stopped.

Anyway, on the day of this rally, I led some religious wearing habits up Madison Avenue at the request of Cardinal O'Connor. He wanted to make sure we were all seated in the front pews of the cathedral. When we arrived, the cathedral had been emptied for a bomb search before the Mass. Can't you just see the police dogs going through the church looking for bombs! I'm glad God has a sense of humor.

By this time, a crowd estimated at forty-five hundred had gathered in front of the cathedral with signs. Perhaps a thousand were demonstrating *in favor* of the church, carrying signs defending Catholic teaching. But the newspapers lumped these counter-demonstrators with those rallying *against* the church.

The demonstrators were not an impressive looking group. Many wore phony miters on which were written obscenities. Many carried outrageous signs. They screamed and yelled, but the demonstration was well-controlled. The police did a marvelous job. A number of the cops greeted me with "Top of the morning, Father," some with egg splattered on their uniform.

A prayerful congregation of thousands had packed the cathedral. I was particularly delighted to see several members of Courage, an organization sponsored by the archdiocese for people with homosexual tendencies who wish to lead a chaste life. I also noticed people from a twelve-step group called Alcoholics Anonymous. Their definition of chastity strikes me right out of the catechism.

Once the liturgy was underway, quiet blanketed the cathedral. Then at the first words of the Cardinal's sermon, demonstrators began yelling and lying down in the center aisle. They handcuffed themselves to the church benches. Vicious screams and cat calls soon filled the sanctuary. After we said one sorrowful mystery of the rosary, the Cardinal continued with the liturgy, while the seminarians distributed a printed copy of his homily.

During the consecration of the Precious Blood, you could almost touch the presence of God. It was an awesome experience. Cardinal O'Connor presided over the liturgy without any sign of anger, but rather with a sense of profound sorrow.

Since the Cardinal did not distribute Holy Communion, I accidentally ended up in his station in the center aisle. I was afraid someone would knock the ciborium from my hands, so I was holding it tightly while distributing Communion.

Suddenly, in front of me stood a young man, dressed in a suitcoat and tie, with short hair neatly combed. He took the host in his hand and held it up. Then he said to me quietly, "This is what I think of your God."

I watched in horror as he crushed the host with his fingers, and let it fall on the floor. Since I was afraid to put down the ciborium, I quickly motioned to the associate at the cathedral, who came over and picked up the particles. The police took the young man into custody.

I was simply astonished. His tone of voice did not fit what he had just done. If someone was going to profane the Holy Eucharist, I wouldn't expect him to do it in the same tone of voice I hear in the confessional. I thought most blasphem went first-class in the wrong direction. Not this fellow seemed frightened to death. I don't know whether h Catholic; I suspect that he was not. But he struck m in a great deal of conflict, not at peace with what h

What a tragedy! But don't worry about God have taught for centuries that since the resurre "hurt" God in himself. Sadly, he can be hurt

I assure you that what is done every day in abortuaries is a far greater offense to God than the profanation of the Holy Eucharist. What shall God say about an attack that kills a child and brings a moral nightmare to those who are responsible?

If a Catholic knowingly desecrates a consecrated host, that person is excommunicated, and only the pope can lift his or her excommunication. If the person who does it is a man, he becomes canonically irregular—meaning he can never be a priest without special permission of the Holy See. If a priest or deacon were to do this, he could never function with Holy Orders for the rest of his life until forgiven by the pope. It is a sin of the same magnitude as laying violent hands on the pope or breaking the seal of confession.

The judge who sentenced this man a year later to twenty-five hours of community service (at an agency of his choice) compared his bravery in attacking oppression to the life of Ghandi. Adding insult to injury in the courts continues.

I wish I knew who that young fellow was. I would send him a copy of my book on chastity, maybe even a couple of audiotapes. He's on a list of people I pray for every day—my own "rogues" gallery of those in great spiritual danger. My list includes people like Madonna, Prince, Ozzie Osborne, and Phil Donahue. Can you imagine how much pain that young man must have been in to behave in such a way?

The newspapers quoted many demonstrators with obviously Irish or Italian names. Several said, "I went to Catholic grade school." That's all right; they may yet be converted and become saints. Don't forget that the soldier who pierced our Lord with the lance while he hung on the cross is venerated as St. Longinus the Centurion. And don't forget St. Paul, who personally presided over "stop the church" rallies of the earliest variety.

We must not be disheartened, but rather strengthened in our faith when we face persecution. We need to be prepared to accept opposition and hostility. We American Catholics are out of practice. In 1928, my own mother was dismissed from her first job because she listed on her application that she was a Roman

Catholic. Eventually, that company was run by Catholics! Things have gotten too easy. We have to get back into shape. We're spiritually flabby.

Our Savior was in St. Patrick's that day. Had I been able to walk out with him after the liturgy onto the cathedral steps and then hear the mob insult him, what do you suppose he would have said? I think Christ would have said exactly what he said about the most terrible sin that was ever committed: *"Father, forgive them; for they know not what they do"* (Lk 23:34).

◆ ◆ ◆

O Lord Jesus Christ, give me the grace to become your true disciple. Let me see ever more clearly that faith in you is not simply a conviction of my mind—but a call to live my life for you and with you.

Your presence as Son of God is all around me. Your presence is to be found in the sacraments, in the Scripture, in the poor and suffering, in the lowly and the dying, even among your enemies where you are betrayed and crucified anew. Send your Holy Spirit to tear aside the veil of material appearances so that I may grow ever more aware of your presence all around me.

Let me welcome you into the center of my poor being just as you came to the house of the publican. Let me seek and find you, recognize and serve you in all who suffer. Give me the grace, O Savior of the world, to bring your presence even to your enemies and to persist faithfully in witnessing to them even when I find it painful to do so. Let me be inspired by your martyrs who constantly call us back to you, our only hope and salvation. Amen.

FOUR

Conversion: Our Struggle against the World

Do not love the world or the things in the world. If any one loves the world, love for the Father is not in him. For all that is in the world, the lust of the flesh and the lust of the eyes and the pride of life, is not of the Father but is of the world. And the world passes away, and the lust of it; but he who does the will of God abides for ever. 1 Jn 2:15-17

T HE PRETTY GIRL IN FRONT OF ME looked too young to be the mother of the baby she held in her arms. Candy's features were Latino, but her last name sounded Italian. When I asked the baby's name, she answered with a big smile: "Emily." I was surprised at such a traditional name. When I asked her about herself, this young girl recounted an all-too-common story.

When Candy was barely two years old, her father had taken her away from her drug-addicted mother. "When I was fifteen, my father and stepmother kicked me out." Where had she lived? Her honest but suspiciously innocent answer seemed to cover over a great deal of suffering and even degradation: "Here and there on the West side." I immediately understood that the girl had been involved in prostitution.

Candy eventually met a boy who promised to marry her. They lived together for awhile and she conceived little Emily. The young couple wanted to get their own place to live, but they didn't have enough money. When the boy decided to take matters into his own hands, he got caught holding up a local liquor store. As a parole violator, he went to jail for seven-and-a-half years. This father-to-be's advice to Candy: "Don't wait for me."

With a baby on the way and no way to provide, the streetwise young woman went to Covenant House for help. After the birth, workers there referred her to Good Counsel Homes, an outreach to homeless mothers partially supported by our little Franciscan community and founded by a dedicated young man named Chris Bell.

Had she been in touch with any of her relatives? No, the girl did not know where her mother was and would not contact her father and stepmother. "Well, you must have other relatives," I said. Grandparents? No. Aunts and uncles, cousins? No. Finally I said, "Candy, everyone has some relatives. You must have someone, someplace in this world."

With a completely innocent expression, this child of sorrow tenderly clutched her little baby. With the most innocent smile, Candy said, "I have Emily." Here was a victim so young in years and already sorely battered.

Our Lord Jesus Christ said that he had come to save the world and would draw all people to himself (Jn 12:32). On other occasions, he identified his adversary as the prince of this world who would be driven out. Jesus warned his disciples that the world would hate them as it had hated him. He goes so far as to say, "If you were of the world, the world would love its own; but because you are not of the world, but I chose you out of the world, therefore the world hates you" (Jn 15:19-20).

How can we understand what Jesus meant by "the world"? On one hand, it means human society, or the whole cosmos that Christ came to sanctify. Candy and Emily are part of that world, and they are also victims of the world's *paganism*.

Today we hardly think of people as pagans. But modern

paganism had trapped this young girl in a world without values, without respect for individuals. In fact, Candy had come into contact with paganism when she first sought help. Before she had gone to Covenant House, "nice" people had all too easily suggested that the best answer was to have an abortion. In fact, the only thing that stood between this girl and an empty life of prostitution was that innocent baby named Emily, who had almost become another lamb sent to the slaughter.

BABYLON IN THE BRONX

The devastation we see at Mount St. Helens or in the Bronx occurs in less obvious fashion all over the world. A new *paganism* grows rampant in the streets of America and in all the cities of industrialized nations. I live in a city that would make Corinth and Babylon blush. The Roman gladiators in full armor might be afraid to walk down some of the streets in our Bronx neighborhood! But in affluent sections of New York, people are victims of an even more insidious paganism that threatens to destroy them and their loved ones.

If you consider that statement extreme, try to take an imaginary trip. Put yourself in the place of a visitor from another planet who walks through the broad and pleasant center of a modern commercial city—like New York, London, Tokyo, or Rome. Would you wonder what kind of alien beings live there?

I am very familiar with the sights and sounds that daily assault one's senses in the Big Apple. From fancy shops to sidewalk vendors, merchants sell things none of us needs. Honking cars, buses, and trucks joust with impatient taxicab drivers, creating a din which makes it almost impossible to think. Hordes of well-dressed pedestrians hustle to reach their next destination, dodging their way through the outstretched hands of homeless beggars.

Our creature from another world would no doubt identify a place of worship here or there—a temple, a cathedral, a church.

But it would probably think that the towering glass buildings on Park Avenue and Wall Street are temples as well. And what of all the green paper being exchanged? It would be even more puzzled by the frenetic dances at the stock market with incredible electronic gadgets providing the rhythm. The greatest of all the local gods would probably appear to this visitor to be money. And yet our visitor could also find people who struggle for other gods such as beauty, power, and prestige.

A film called *The Dead Poet's Society* intriguingly depicts the struggle between the search for godless beauty on one hand and greed on the other. In an upper class boys' academy—where parents send their sons not only to learn discipline but also how to make lots of money—religious traditions have been reduced to merely vague references and occasional pious hymns.

In order to stir his students to search for spiritual values and deeper meaning, an English professor passionately throws his energy into opening their minds to the sublime heights of poetry. He happens to be a disciple of the old classical paganism, as expressed by the best of the Romantic poets like Byron, Shelley, and Keats, whose verses reflect noble ideals of bravery and decency.

This teacher's unorthodox methods include ordering his students to rip out pages of dull poetry books, as well as having them stand on top of their desks to recite poetic lines of their own making. The academy's administration is not amused, much less tolerant of such blatant disregard for tradition, discipline, and decorum.

The father of one student seems totally invested in his son's becoming a wealthy surgeon. But the unconventional English instructor awakens this boy's ardent desire to become an actor, to pursue something that goes beyond money to a certain beauty, a certain sense of culture, even though it is without God. The boy's father adamantly demands his son withdraw from such foolish and impractical pursuits as the theater.

This film holds out no God, no Christ, no hope. The boy can see no avenue of escape from his dilemma. He is crushed between two paganisms: the *old classical paganism of beauty* and the *modern paganism of power and wealth.* The distraught boy finally takes his own life.

The tragedy is that such a drama frequently unfolds in real life. How often are young people forced to accept the new gods of corruption and money? How often are our children driven by the desire to "be somebody"? How often do we ourselves nibble at the tempting leaves of paganism? How often do we fail to appreciate the full meaning of salvation?

Paganism as I am using the term simply means what is indicated by the first commandment: *making oneself into a false god.* Putting ourselves first, and helping and encouraging other people to put themselves first.

Candy was thrown out of her home because her father and stepmother thought she was too much trouble. She was sexually abused because her customers put themselves and their lust first. Her boyfriend put himself first when he held up the liquor store. Candy met some of paganism's present-day apostles when those nice people offered to help her kill her unborn child. And even now, paganism would condemn her for bringing her baby into the world.

Notice that I am not identifying paganism as the other religions of the world. At their best, these religions reflect an honest attempt to find the real God. As all human belief systems tend to do, they sometimes create gods in their own image—an image that is proud and self-seeking—like the god-kings of Egypt. But paganism as I am using the term can be operative in the lives of Christians, even those who see themselves as committed disciples of Christ. We all need to examine our consciences about unconscious paganism. You can easily identify it when you notice that you are putting yourself first.

DOES PAGANISM ENTER YOUR LIFE?

Does paganism enter your life? It certainly enters mine—by anger, by judgmental attitudes toward individuals, by placing myself above other people. Haven't you acted like a pagan sometime in the last couple of days? Come on now, be honest! If a driver tosses his coins and misses the toll gate, would you immediately become a raging pagan at having to wait? I've done that. We often treat strangers with utter coldness; we even behave this way toward our relatives and friends when things don't go our way. Ancient pagans had a saying that sums up this attitude: "Homo homini lupus"—man unto man a wolf, or every one a wolf to his or her neighbor.

Have I been influenced by paganism? Without a doubt. I used to kid myself that I didn't have the same prejudices as many others. In the little town of Caldwell, New Jersey, where I grew up, black people lived in a small segregated section called Francisco Street. I was never aware of unkind actions toward them, but the black people were certainly pushed around and taken advantage of. When I was twelve years old, I asked myself this question on Christmas Eve: where would Jesus have been born if he had come to our town? I can remember clearly thinking that he would have been born on Francisco Street. Why? Because Jesus was born among the very poor. So I made up my mind right then that I would not be prejudiced against black people.

I often heard of anti-semitism, but I grew up without harboring it myself. One of my first spiritual advisors was a wise, aged Jewish tailor. I used to feel that I was talking to a prophet when I stood in the window of the French Dry Cleaners and talked with Mr. Graff.

As I look back, I realize I was raised without ethnic prejudices. I have a love-hate relationship with New York City precisely because this teeming metropolis is home to every conceivable ethnic group. The city both helps and destroys them. I have over the years worked with people of most unusual ethnic combinations—for example, a brother and sister who were Jordanian-Columbians.

However, the very real prejudices I do harbor are much more deep-seated, and thus much more pagan. Do you know whom I have a burning prejudice against? People who don't like me, or ignore me, or think that what I have to say is not worthwhile. I'm not particular. If you like me, it doesn't matter to me who or what you are. But if you don't appreciate me or what I have to say, a little pagan quickly rears his ugly head, full of prejudices and hurt feelings.

Perhaps you thought priests were holier than that. Don't I wish! The road ahead of me is still filled with too many of my own pagan shrines and obstacles—some, boulders and mountains; and others, pebbles and molehills. One's sanctification is not accomplished quickly, once we say "I do" to the Lord. It means a daily—even hourly—struggle to return to God, to take the next good step, to keep going and keep growing.

Everyone of us needs conversion from paganism. The first step of discipleship is to overcome our paganism by following the commandments of the Old Testament and the beatitudes of the New Testament. Moses and the prophets, Jesus, the apostles and the evangelists—these are our guides in our ongoing struggle for conversion. Moreover, we have many brothers and sisters in Christ to lend a hand when we feel overcome.

CONVERSION FROM WHAT?

I have frequently mentioned ongoing conversion in my books and tapes. Some people ask me, "Conversion from what?" Most Catholics would say conversion from *sin*, but that's too simple an answer. Others think we need to be converted from *weakness*, but that's not quite precise either. God assists us out of our weakness once we acknowledge our powerlessness and ask for help.

Most of us need to be converted from the root of paganism, which is our *unbelief*. Even if we basically believe, our faith is usually riddled with holes. Our belief in God is like a leaky boat from which we have to keep bailing water during the storms of life. Jagged rocks and hidden icebergs can puncture our flimsy craft, while worldly barnacles slow us down. Once the waves swell and crash over the stern, we realize we're not the spiritual giants we once imagined.

Most people who read this book are believing Christians who struggle against their pagan inclinations. So conversion from what? The answer is not from unbelief itself or from explicitly pagan values, but from the subtle and insidious influences of modern paganism. Peter Kreeft describes our peril in this way:

> The most serious threat to Christianity today is not any one of the other great religions of the world such as Islam or Buddhism. Nor is it simple atheism, which has no depth, no mass appeal, and no roots, tradition, or staying power. Rather, it is a religion most of us think is dead. The religion is paganism, and it is very much alive.
>
> There is an Old Paganism and a New Paganism. What holds both together under the same name is a vague old religion, a popular religious alternative to Christianity without a supernaturally revealed creed, code, or cult. Paganism is simply the natural gravity of the human spirit, the religious line of least resistance, religion in its natural, fallen state.[1]

The Gospels tell the story of men and women who, once converted, were being cleansed of their pagan attitudes. The process of ongoing conversion was necessary even though most of them had been raised as strict Jews with a conscious abhorrence of paganism.

Acceptance of Jesus Christ as our personal Savior is only the beginning of a *lifelong* process of conversion. God calls us to a *constant conversion*, a daily process of cleansing. We must pray for the conversion of all pagans, starting with our own radical transformation. Our conversion is never complete until we enter heaven.

Every human being begins life without grace, as a little pagan. When we leave our mothers' wombs, we are not baptized and we have original sin. Every newborn is in need of conversion. Each of us starts with no revelation from God, yet we all soon sense we need to believe in something beyond ourselves.

I was born a pagan and became a Catholic about two weeks later when my parents had me baptized. Although a Christian for more than half a century, I still fall prey to the pervasive influence of neo-paganism. I still face the daily struggle of conversion, trying to conform my heart and mind to the ways of God.

God spoke through the prophet Isaiah about the distance separating God and humanity: "For as the heavens are higher than the earth, so are my ways higher than your ways and my thoughts than your thoughts" (Is 55:9). Yet we all tend to reduce God to our own levels and forget the chasm which can be crossed only by the saving grace of Jesus Christ. Instead of falling on our faces in worship and humility, we can be easily sidetracked by relying on our own flimsy efforts to please God.

Many people find it difficult to escape from their own paganism. It might be a help to recall that modern paganism was preceded by an old paganism. Most of us had some sort of tribal paganism in our family trees not too long ago.

If you are descended from northern European stocks—Irish, German, English, Nordic, or Slav—your relatives were converted from paganism anywhere from a thousand to fifteen hundred years ago. If you're of Italian or Greek extraction, the apostles and their successors were working on your ancestors for about three hundred years after the resurrection. If you're Jewish, you are historically a step or two ahead of the rest of us. Your ancestors were converted from paganism starting with Abraham about eighteen hundred years before Christ. But if you recall from the Old Testament, the Israelites suffered many lapses into paganism.

Maybe you are African American and can go back only a couple hundred years ago to find paganism actively practiced by your relatives. And don't forget the paganism of those who enslaved them in Christian America. No doubt some of the readers of this book were raised in an explicitly anti-religious environment filled with modern paganism.

Whoever you are and whatever your family background, turn your mind back to when you were born. You, too, started your earthly journey as a pagan. One elderly lady told me that she was brought to this country from Italy when she was only a few weeks old. Her grandma met her family at the boat and took them immediately to church. The baby had to be baptized before they got home. She didn't want a pagan in her house!

Pope John XXIII's mother had about twenty children and resolved that not one of them would spend a single day without being baptized. When John was born at almost eleven at night, she sent one of the family to get the parish priest out of bed, and was present at the baptism herself—having delivered the future pope forty-five minutes earlier. That may be overdoing it a bit, but her absolute resolve helps us to remember that we all started out as pagans not so long ago.

Paganism often enters the life of the church, just as it did in the life of ancient Israel. That is because, yesterday as today, all are born pagans and are in need of being baptized, justified, delivered, and constantly called to conversion by Christ. How often does each of us hear whispered in the ears of our souls: "Did God say...?" (Gn 3:1). How often do we listen and take this temptation seriously? How often do we proceed on the treacherous terrain of doubting God's commands?

Our Christianity can easily shift off course toward our pagan roots. The old paganism revived many times during the Renaissance and the so-called Enlightenment. The Romantic period in England produced a variety of poets, some of them deeply religious and even committed Christians, like Sir Walter Scott, Tennyson, Longfellow, and Wordsworth. But others were beguiled by paganism—Byron, Keats, and Shelley. Their neo-paganism had a sense of beauty, right and wrong, judgment, tragedy, and the divine—but attributed these qualities to the wrong source. Their neo-paganism never went beyond self, like the well-intentioned but misguided teacher in *The Dead Poet's Society.*

A poet named Algernon Swinburne belonged to an old Catholic family which had abandoned its long-held faith after enduring centuries of persecution in England. Swinburne penned extremely paganistic poetry, including an attack on Christ in his poem on Julian the Apostate: "You have conquered, O pale Galilean, and the world has grown gray at your breath." That's what those demonstrators were really shouting outside St. Patrick's Cathedral, only not so poetically.

Some relics in church history reflect this preoccupation with paganism. Have you heard of the Tivoli Gardens in Rome? A fascinating architectural masterpiece, its ornate fountains below the edge of a cliff shoot streams of water twenty or thirty feet in the air. Immense quantities of it are transported completely by the power of gravity, without any mechanical assistance. But what decorates the Tivoli Gardens? Statues of nymphs and satyrs, of pagan gods and goddesses. I contemplated knocking them down to put up statues of St. Elizabeth Seton or Mother Cabrini. But you know what is really disturbing? The Tivoli Gardens were commissioned by a Renaissance cardinal.

ARE YOU A PAGAN?

Paganism today is not simply an ancient aberration. Rather than bothering with religious sensibilities such as beauty, morality, punishment, or tragedy, *neo-pagans are caught up in embracing plain, old-fashioned materialism*. We human beings tend to think we are more important or better than others because of what we possess. We often focus on accumulating more goods, bigger and better houses, newer automobiles. Few people give shopping on Sunday a second thought. Flying first-class or jumping on a cruise ship and having people wait on us is utterly enticing.

"Give me... I want... Let me have... We'll go first-class... Everybody can wait on us... All we need is money." Do you recognize those themes in your own life? We often buy what we don't need and cling to what we have. Then we give to the needy from what is leftover. Here are some clues for identifying modern paganism in our own lives.

Human beings are seen as objects to be used and then cast aside. In times past, pagan philosophers retained some sense of decency, but today that is fading fast. No issue demonstrates this pragmatic disregard more clearly than the pro-choice, pro-life debate. Nothing is absolute if you can take a human life simply because it is convenient or expedient to do so.

Some ancient pagans, like the Romans, were so horrified by infanticide that when they took Carthage, they killed all four hundred priests of a pagan temple where children were sacrificed. By comparison, I heard of a Catholic woman, active in pro-life, who wanted her daughter to have an abortion! She never showed her face around the pro-life movement again, but she continued to be a very opinionated Catholic.

People have reverted to being gods themselves, deciding when to take their own lives or the lives of loved ones who are suffering too much pain. The recent publication of *Final Exit* by Derek Humphrey, the president of England's Hemlock Society, has fueled the euthanasia and suicide debate. This slim volume, which details various methods of self-assisted suicide has proved to be surprisingly popular. Even the young and healthy seem morbidly curious about their options in case of need.

This kind of paganism is violent. It is anti-human, appealing to our basest instincts. I'm not talking about the paganism of the Romans, Greeks, and Nordic tribes, or of those who sought the one, true God and later embraced the good news of Jesus Christ. The most vicious paganism often festers in those who have been sealed by holy Baptism and have then turned their backs on Christ. The evening television will bring you a number of commentators and entertainers who were raised Catholics or Protestants but now make war on the teachings of Christ.

The new paganism has a blatant disregard for the presence of Christ in others and their essential value and dignity as God's children. How many times in history has Christ been defended in paganistic ways? When the crusaders took Jerusalem, they killed the Moslems and Jews in the name of Christ! They were acting like pagans, covered with blood. How many people consider themselves devout believers and yet support governmental policies filled with hatred, violence, and vindictiveness? How many times, even in our defense of Christianity, do we act in an unchristian way?

In the past, how many Americans considered themselves devout Christians, while wholeheartedly supporting slavery and segregation? And today, how do we Christians treat those of a different color or race? How do we treat the poor? Do we see Christ in them?

As society becomes more pagan, it will return to outright slavery. You watch! Even in a democracy, subtle ways exist in which the powerful can control the weak, making them their chattels, their beasts of burden. Take an American dollar, fold it into ten sections, and cut off the tenth part. That represents the capital earned in the United States by slaves for the first ninety years of our existence as a nation. Ten percent of the basic capital of the United States is estimated as having come from slavery.

Is slavery in America really a thing of the past? We still have all kinds of prejudices by which we treat other people as less than human because of their race, creed, color, circumstances, pathology, weakness, or handicap. Sometimes we reject someone just because we don't like the expression on his or her face!

In most underdeveloped countries a huge underclass is growing in an alarming way: masses of unwanted people, many of them descendants of the victims of slavery or the exploitations of Latin American countries by American business interests. The growing gap between the rich and poor is rooted in paganism. When the poor got out of hand in ancient Rome, the ruling class gave them bread and circuses. Modern society offers them drugs and television.

The riots in Los Angeles following the Rodney King verdict in 1992 were a volcanic eruption of racial and social discontent. People all over the country looked on in disbelief after the jury found the four white policemen not guilty of excessive force in the beating of a black motorist. Feeling powerless and betrayed by the justice system, revengeful mobs launched days of killing, burning, and looting. Over forty people died in the worst civil violence of this decade. Pagan values led to pagan responses.

Paganism lacks a sense of the divine and transcendent in human lives. Pagan gods were projections of the religious and personal needs of human beings. These gods, then and now, are made in the image of humankind. They have eyes and see not, ears and hear not. Christians do not follow a god of their making. We follow a real God who came down from heaven. He does not need to ask our needs and desires, even less our opinions. Christ asks that we believe and follow him.

Even when we are trying to be faithful, we live among people who are under the influence of paganism—in our own families, among our friends, in our parishes. Do we put Christ first? Are our spiritual lives just a consolation we turn to when times are tough? In Kreeft's words, many people worship the "blob god," a god made in the image of the "Pillsbury Dough Boy."

This new god that does not seek anything beyond itself, is perhaps manifested in the New Age Movement. Having been lured by the promise of spiritual power, healing, and a richer life, its adherents are ensnared by age-old superstitions. New Age devotees sometimes borrow the trappings of by-gone romantic paganism, like talking to crystals. Such wacky pastimes as attempting to contact the spirits of the dead (called channeling), astrology, numerology, and psychic communication are growing in popularity. Wicca, an old English term for witchcraft, invites people to worship an earth mother or goddess. What the New Age Movement is essentially saying is that humankind is an end in itself and thus is its own god.

Neo-paganism has no sense of the beautiful or the transcendent. The nihilism of much modern art provides many examples, such as the "dada" art of Andy Warhol. Modern art can have beauty and meaning, but too often it is the art of the ugly, the pedestrian, assembled into meaningless forms. The message seems to be that human life itself is devoid of meaning.

Modern paganism places supreme value on this present secular life, the visible world. We all share a tendency to water down the transcendent message of the gospel and the mysteries of Christ. Perhaps without even realizing it, we try to make Jesus into a nice man who fits into our secular values. How many among us have fully embraced his hard sayings, like loving our enemies and giving away what we have to the poor?

I have watched professors at religious universities quibble, so that they proclaim Christ in the weakest of terms. The task of the theologian is to interpret revelation in a way that can be comprehended and embraced. It is not the task of a theologian simply to present revelation in a way that can be easily accepted. A present-day anomaly is the success of those who present a straight-forward, challenging Christianity. In contrast, those who present a diluted, semi-pagan form of Christianity often have difficulty attracting a serious audience.

Several secular universities in the United States have very effective Newman Clubs. The priests who oversee them are often older men who have a crisp and sharp dedication to Christian teaching and Catholic dogma. Not having been compromised by the environment in which they live, these religious have gradually surrounded themselves with committed groups of faculty and students who are also not afraid to be countercultural. A number of these Newman clubs produce one or two vocations to the priesthood every year.

On the other hand, some large Catholic universities produce almost no vocations at all. In fact, many of the priests who are faculty members of these universities eventually end up leaving the priesthood and even abandoning their Christian faith. I see these examples as clear evidence that intellectually kowtowing to the paganistic environment in which we live is not only morally offensive but also ineffective in presenting the truths of salvation.

The new paganism embraces a relativistic morality. This new paganism of materialism and consumerism reflects no absolute moral standards. It is relativistic, subjective, and pragmatic. Success can be wrongly defined by the values of those around us. Good in our world is often defined by that which is convenient or pleasurable. Evil becomes whatever is inconvenient.

Many Christians feel like second-class citizens because they are not trendy or are less successful. We constantly apologize for our faith and pussy-foot around our deepest beliefs. If everyone else is doing it, the actions of the majority begin to make it right, or at least acceptable.

Modern paganism can even prevent the believer from standing up for the downtrodden or working for a change in legislation that goes against the supreme law of God. Many have come to believe that our culture is intrinsically Christian, that whatever the government or the Supreme Court or television says must be the same as Christianity. Thus, divine revelation can become riddled with the termites of pseudo-democracy. Protesting against abortion is one way believers have of laying their lives on the line to defend those of the unborn and to change wicked laws. How many of us are doing just that?

Modern paganism is sensed in a sense of meaninglessness and desperation about our lives. If you're feeling hopeless because the church seems to be losing ground, even going under, exerting less influence, becoming dominated—then you may be under the spell of paganism. As Christians we cannot become too discouraged because we look forward to the heavenly kingdom, no matter what circumstances we encounter on earth. God has promised victory for his people in the end.

Even in deep suffering, the believer can know a peace that goes beyond this world, a satisfaction, a joy that no one can take away. St. Paul says that we glory in the cross of our Lord Jesus Christ, for "if we have died with him, we shall also live with him; if we endure, we shall also reign with him" (2 Tm 2:11-12).

Paganism eventually will give itself away by showing its true colors. It inevitably comes to a dead end; it wears out. During this very century, the most atrocious, vicious form of paganism since Nero, took control over the heart of Europe. As Carl Jung noted during Hitler's rise to power, after two thousand years of Christian education, a dark paganism so blatant it could not be ignored, was sweeping away Christian culture.

Christian education has done all that is humanly possible, but it has not been enough. Too few people have experienced the divine image as the innermost possession of their own souls. Christ only meets them from without, never from within the soul; that is why dark paganism still reigns there, a paganism which, now in a form so blatant that it can no longer be denied and now in all too threadbare disguise, is swamping the world of so-called Christian culture....[2]

What were the Nazis if not quintessential pagans? Rosenburg, their half-baked philosopher, even wrote a book about the revival of paganism called *The Myth of the Twentieth Century.* Heinrich Himmler, head of the dreaded SS, dabbled with paganistic symbols like rune stones. The Nazis even established pagan ceremonies to replace the Sacraments of Baptism and Marriage. The New Age, although at this point less vicious, is currently developing its own rites of passage.

You and I need constantly to root out the new paganism from our lives. Keeping oneself unaffected by pagan values has been the struggle of Christians ever since Roman times. Every day I look at my own life and see evidence of materialism and self-centeredness. I must admit that the old paganism of the beautiful and the mysterious is somewhat more attractive to me personally, but the new paganism of the ugly and the material-istic can be even more destructive.

True Christianity inevitably clashes head-on with paganistic culture. Remember Jesus warning us that the world would hate us (Jn 17:11-19). Today we can see the growing spread of anti-Catholicism, the trust in superstition, and openly paganistic forms of worship and ritual like Wicca. All of them are unscriptural projections of people's needs on to God.

A young relative was relating to me recently that she was told in a Catholic academy that God is a woman. God is not a woman, believe me. God is not a man either. God is a *spirit*. But God chose to use masculine images in divine revelation. Our Savior was born into this world as a male. I don't know why. Maybe God felt sorry for us men because women have more abilities. Maybe he chose the numerical minority. Any attempt to create a god in our own image is a pitiful travesty. Whenever we change what is revealed by God to suit our fancy, we take a step toward paganism.

SEEING IN A GLASS DARKLY

Paganism clouds our ability to perceive clearly and appreciate the full meaning of salvation. We can better understand modern paganism if we briefly consider its roots. Classical paganism is a religion in which two elements are operative. The first is very important and God-given: a spiritual hunger, a need for God, a need to hold and find something that goes beyond this world, a need for a hope that does not perish.

The second we have already considered—namely the tendency to think of God as like oneself. The pagan gods, especially the Greco-Roman variety, were projections of many human vices and instinctual desires. That's why the pagan gods of Greece and Rome were not terribly well-behaved. Nordic pagan gods often represented human projections of fear and terror. Those gods are not so far from us. We still call the days of the week by their names: Wodin's Day, Thor's Day, Frei's Day. The month of January is named after the Greek god of the door, Janis, because it stands at the beginning of the year.

Almost all pagan religions upheld some moral principles undergirded by the belief that human beings would be punished for misdeeds, often severely and mercilessly. At the same time, this pagan morality could be very relativistic, disregarding this or that serious immorality according to what the specific culture projected onto its gods. With all its shortcomings, the old paganism presented a strange kind of absolute, objective morality. While not comprehensively including every wrong, it usually covered the basic principles of natural law. At its best, paganism was a natural religion developed by people who were not guided by divine revelation.

The punitive quality of pagan morality admitted no excuses such as ignorance and weakness. If one was innocently guilty of wrongdoing, one was stuck with the consequences. Many victims of the pagan gods were simply at the wrong place at the wrong time.

For instance, one of the most powerful of the Greeks' myths concerns the tragedy of King Oedipus. Without his knowledge, this man married his mother. Calamities came upon his city-state: hailstorms, hurricanes, tornadoes, earthquakes. No one could understand why the gods were angry. Finally, an old servant woman who had raised the king told the queen that she had unknowingly married her son after her first husband was killed.

In the last scene we see King Oedipus stricken with grief and remorse. As a penance, he has torn out his eyes so that he may never again see his children, who are both his siblings and his offspring. He and the whole country suffered cruel punishment from the gods—even though the king himself was innocent of willful sin.

Later Jewish and Christian beliefs took into account extenuating circumstances, the mercy of God, and the possibility of forgiveness. The God of revelation does not need to exact some terrible penalty. God can and does forgive. After Christianity offered this alternative, the ancient pagans often mocked their gods and rejoiced at their downfall. But remnants of paganism's severe morality remain.

We find an example of leftover paganism in the Old Testament story of Jephtha the Gileadite (Jgs 11). Jephtha was a mighty warrior, but the son of a harlot who had been driven away from the family home by his half-brothers. Desirous of victory in battle against the Ammonites so that he could return home as a leader, Jephtha made a rash vow to the Lord. If he won, then whoever came forth from the doors of his house to meet him when he returned after battle would be sacrificed to God.

The mighty warrior was overwhelmed with great sorrow when his beautiful sixteen-year-old daughter came running down the path to greet him. But Jephtha believed himself to be irrevocably bound by his vow. His only child agreed to be sacrificed—with the request that she be allowed to wander in the mountains with her girlfriends for two months to bewail her virginity. And so it came to pass.

Does that fit the knowledge we have of God? Of course not. Later books of Jewish Scripture as well as the New Testament present a much different and more highly developed picture of God. The Deuterocanonical books, written much later, depict a much gentler, benign, forgiving, and understanding image of God. But the early Israelites, like Jephtha, still harbored misunderstandings of God's love and mercy because of their recent passage from paganism and because divine revelation was still incomplete.

Don't be too ready to shake your head at this account and mutter, "tsk, tsk." We ourselves come under the influence of this kind of paganism. Sometimes we can't believe God has forgiven us even though we have confessed our sin. Such so-called scrupulosity has an element of paganism. "Oh, did I confess that the right way?" Suppose you didn't. If you did your best, so what? "Oh, but I won't be forgiven." Are you relating to the Old Testament picture of God without considering his further revelation of himself in the New Testament?

For example, how do we relate to our own enemies or to the enemies of religion? In the Old Testament, they usually go to hell in a speedboat. But the New Testament emphasizes the mercy of God. Christ prays, "Father, forgive them." The Good Shepherd leaves the ninety-nine to look for the one who is lost.

Do you find it strange that God's image seems to change from the Old Testament to the New Testament? Of course,

God is the same from age to age, but our understanding is always limited. Our Lord came to this earth to reveal more to us about who God really is. We all have limited notions of God. Who can fathom the depth of the knowledge or love of God?

Ancient Greco-Roman paganism fell apart when it came into contact with the teachings of Jesus Christ. Because he was both divine and human, he brought heaven and earth together. With his humanity, there was divinity; with his divinity, humanity. The distance between God and humanity was closed by this divine but humble carpenter who lived among us as a common man.

The pagans surrounded their gods with awe, sometimes placating them with human sacrifice. What fear God had inspired was now moderated by his love as manifested in his divine Son. Here was a God whom you could call by the first intelligible sound any human being utters: "Abba" or "Dada." How plain, how simple, how beautiful, how merciful, how loving, how holy.

In Christ, the profound needs of humankind were finally and ultimately fulfilled. The pagan mysteries were undone and replaced by the sacraments, signs of divine love in a material world. The fear of the cosmos was dispelled because the elements could be seen as displaying the power of God. In countless ways, the religious longing of the human race expressed in paganism found fulfillment in Christianity.

HOW DID JESUS RELATE TO THE PAGANS?

Our Lord lived much of his life either among pagans—as he did in Egypt as a child—or on the edges of the pagan world where it encountered the unified culture of observant Jews. Both Nazareth and the Sea of Galilee were home to many non-believers. In fact, the city next to Capernaum was a pagan city named after the Roman emperor, Tiberius.

Jesus instructed his apostles to make disciples of all the nations. All of humanity needed conversion and healing. We see Jesus often reaching out to pagans, calling the Gentiles or peoples of other nations, with kindness and favor. The miracle of the demoniac in the country of the Gerasenes took place among the pagans (Lk 8:26-39).

One of Our Lord's most startling miracles was the raising of the servant boy belonging to the centurion of Capernaum. This man graciously declines Jesus' offer to come to his house, saying, "I am not worthy to have you come under my roof; but only say the word, and my servant will be healed. For I am a man under authority, with soldiers under me; and I say to one, 'Go,' and he goes, and to another, 'Come,' and he comes, and to my slave, 'Do this,' and he does it" (Mt 8:8-9). Jesus marvels at the centurion's faith and immediately grants his request. He was probably one of the "God-fearing" pagans, someone who believed in the God of the Jews, but had been advised against formally converting because of the burdens of the Mosaic law.

A seemingly harsh interaction takes place when a Canaanite woman begs Jesus for mercy on her daughter who was possessed by a demon (Mt 15:22-28). The mother would not be rebuffed by his disciples or by Jesus' claim to be sent only to the Jews. When she kneels before him, our Lord excuses himself by what sounds like a popular saying of the day: "It is not fair to take the children's bread and throw it to the dogs." The woman boldly answers, "Yes, Lord, yet even the dogs eat the crumbs that fall from their master's table." Seeing her great faith, Jesus then healed her daughter (Mt 15:22-28). I have always believed that this interchange is best understood when recited with the wry humor I have observed among the old Jewish immigrants from Europe.

BEING A CHRISTIAN IN A PAGAN WORLD

How should *we* respond to the pagans of our day? First of all, we should remember that a great many of them—even those who are baptized or have received other sacraments—have not been well-taught, or perhaps not taught at all. Many are innocent victims of the tumultuous wave of modern paganism. St. Augustine—himself snared in such a trap as a young man—referred to pagan values as a *tidal wave.*

We must prayerfully place them in the hands of God. They may be your relatives, perhaps your child, siblings, spouse, or parent. With prayer and the patient preaching of the gospel by your own good example, these lost souls may yet be brought to Christ. Jesus himself admonishes us to do the works of God while it is still day (Jn 9:4). We must be patient and kind so that those around us may see the face of Christ and come to know his healing touch.

At the same time, we must not become self-righteous. Remember that we all fall short of the commands of God; we are all in need of ongoing conversion. We have seen that every one of us must deal with the influences of paganism in our own lives. Our own struggles should keep us humble and compassionate toward others.

One of the most subtle paganistic attitudes to which Christians often succumb is judging others. St. Augustine speaks of true repentance and avoiding judgment of other people in a sermon on Psalm 51, considered to be David's prayer of repentance after having arranged the death of Uriah, the Hittite, in order to marry his wife, Bathsheba:

"I acknowledge my transgression," says David, "if I admit my fault then you, O God, will pardon it." Let us never assume that if we lead good lives we will be without sin; our lives should be praised only when we continue to beg for pardon. But men are hopeless creatures, and the less they concentrate on their own sins, the more interested they become in the sins of others. They seek to criticize, not to correct. Unable to excuse themselves, they are ready to accuse others.

This was not the way that David showed us how to pray and make amends to God, when he said: "I acknowledge my transgression, and my sin is ever before me." He did not concentrate on other people's sins; he turned his thoughts upon himself. He did not merely stroke the surface, but he plunged inside and went down deep within himself. He did not spare himself, and therefore was not impudent in asking to be spared....

"You will take no delight in burnt offerings," David says. If you will not take delight in burnt offerings, will you remain without sacrifice? Not at all. *A sacrifice to God is a contrite spirit; God does not despise a contrite and humble heart.*

You now have the offering you are to make. No need to examine the herd, no need to outfit ships and travel to the most remote provinces in search of incense. Search within your heart for what is pleasing to God. Your heart must be crushed. Are you afraid that it might perish so? You have the reply: "Create a clean heart in me, O God." For a clean heart to be created, the unclean one must be crushed.

We should be displeased with ourselves when we commit sin, for sin is displeasing to God. Sinful though we are, let us at least be like God in this, that we are displeased at what displeases him. In some measure then you will be in harmony with God's will, because you find displeasing in yourself what is abhorrent to your Creator.[3]

These powerful words of St. Augustine express the attitude of repentance that should characterize the life of the disciple. Indeed, the only appropriate attitude for any believing Christian is repentance, even joyful repentance, but repentance nonetheless.

OUR LORD'S COMPASSION TOWARD SIMPLE BELIEVERS

Pagans can be identified by an attitude of self-importance. This is an unchristian stance, as is self-righteousness. Some very poor Jews like the shepherds in the fields were unable to enter the temple because they were ritually impure. The Pharisees despised these poor huddling masses, which included the man born blind who was healed by Jesus' instruction to wash himself in the pool of Siloam. When he is hauled in front of the Pharisees for questioning, they deride Jesus' act of kindness because it had been done on the sabbath.

"This man is not from God, for he does not keep the sabbath.... How can a man who is a sinner do such signs?" (Jn 9:16). When the poor man still insists that he was healed by Jesus, they revile him by saying, "You were born in utter sin, and would you teach us?" (Jn 9:34). Yet this man, like his revilers, was born a Jew.

Many people these days have been baptized but have had little contact with real Christianity. They are ignorant, perhaps through no fault of their own, with little understanding of the teaching of the gospel. We must be even more patient in calling them to conversion. One never hears Mother Teresa reproaching those who are ignorant or poorly instructed. She shows patience, kindness, and forbearance toward them.

As a priest, I often face the tough question of how to respond to someone who professes faith in the midst of paganism. One afternoon my phone rang and it was a boy named José. "Padre," he said, "I want you to baptize my kid."

I replied, "José, I didn't know you were married."

José shot back, "I ain't. But I got a kid."

"Why, José," I wanted to know, "are you not married?"

"Mirelda and me ain't ready yet."

I had to agree with him on that point. I learned that Mirelda was a simple country girl from an uneducated black family. "Is she Catholic?" I asked.

"No, but she likes Catholics," he responded. I had already figured that out.

I pointed out to José that I could baptize his child only if he was practicing his faith and would guarantee that the child would be brought up as a Catholic. José seemed startled. Of course, he was a Catholic! He had been an altar boy; he went to Mass several Sundays every year, like Christmas, Palm Sunday, and Easter. He even stopped into church to pray now and then. And his girlfriend was interested in becoming a Catholic.

This presented quite a dilemma. Priests can't just baptize

children because their parents want a nice rite of passage for them. There must be some genuine belief and commitment to seeing that the child is brought up in the Catholic faith.

Feeling torn, I mulled over José's request. I finally told him that I would baptize the baby. When I arrived for the Baptism, Mirelda's family was gathered at a large old country church built by Irish immigrants a hundred years before. They were simple, good folk. I took them through the church and explained the scenes in the stained glass windows, the statues, who the saints were, and finally the presence of Christ in the Holy Eucharist. Impressed, they knelt before the tabernacle as I led them in a prayer. I'm sure I could have baptized them all that day.

After baptizing the little baby, I returned to the sacristy still haunted by a lingering doubt as to whether I had done the right thing. As I put my head down on the vesting bench, the words from Our Lady's magnificat echoed in my mind: "He has put down the mighty from their thrones, and exalted those of low degree; he has filled the hungry with good things, and the rich he has sent empty away" (Lk 1:52-53). I suddenly realized that perhaps baptizing that little baby was the very thing my salvation hung upon—because I had done something for the least and the lowest.

A few weeks later, I had an occasion to meet with Mother Teresa. I have learned from experience to back into delicate matters with Mother Teresa because she can be very direct, so I carefully explained the case while leaving the impression that the Baptism was yet to be carried out. What should I do?

Mother Teresa said to me, "Poor Father, you are only a priest. Why take such heavy burdens on yourself? Would you deprive one of God's little children of holy Baptism and the grace of salvation?"

I responded by saying that the child's parents were not "active members of the faith community." They didn't go to church every Sunday. Mother Teresa looked at me very wryly and said, "Father, from what you have told me, this little child is so poor that God himself is her Father and *he* goes to church every day."

Perhaps it would be helpful to recall this story of José and Mirelda when you are troubled by people who seem half-pagan. What did our Lord say about them? He said they were like sheep without a shepherd and he had compassion on them (Mk 6:34).

HOW SHOULD WE RESPOND TO THE MILITANT PAGANS?

What about militant pagans like the ones yelling and screaming in St. Patrick's Cathedral during that anti-church rally in New York City? What better attitude than the one shown by the believers attending that liturgy: an attitude of *sorrow*. Such a noble sentiment is almost impossible to attack. We must give unbelievers a worthy example. Returning the screams of blasphemers only heats up the rhetoric.

If God can put up with you and me, he can put up with a lot of people! Jesus commands us to forgive others, as he has forgiven us and them. Do you remember the parable about the unforgiving steward in Matthew 18? This man, who owed ten thousand talents, implored the king for patience. After being forgiven his debt, this same man seized a fellow servant by the throat and demanded the one hundred denarii owed him. Keep in mind that a talent was more than fifteen years' wages of a laborer; a denarius was a day's wage. The king reprimands the wicked servant, saying, "Should not you have had mercy on your fellow servant, as I had mercy on you?" (Mt 18:33). Jesus is speaking to us about our need to forgive others, just as God has forgiven us.

Finally, there are those who come by their paganism quite legitimately. Many belong to another major world religion like Buddhism or Hinduism. The church teaches us to respect the truth in such non-Christian religions. Buddhists or Hindus usually seem to know something about the one, true God, but have not heard or accepted the fullness of the good news of

Christ. Let us continually pray that they will come to know the love of Jesus. Let us reach out to them in love and compassion, and respect their sincere search for the living God.

THE LITTLE SISTERS OF JESUS

As paganism grows stronger and stronger in the days to come, what shall we do? The answers are in the Gospels and Epistles. We are called to live in a way that bears witness to the love of Christ, holding fast to the precious truths of our salvation.

Let me share a touching story about such a witness of love from my visit to the Little Sisters of Jesus who live at the harbor of Aberdeen in Hong Kong. They made their home on a Chinese junk, one of those little boats handed down from generation to generation. I happened to arrive as a tropical storm was being predicted.

If stormy weather is expected during the night, each family ties its junk to the next one so they won't crash into each other. Eventually, the whole harbor bobs up and down together like one big boat. Even in good weather, people are allowed to walk from one boat to the other as a matter of Oriental courtesy. If your home is several boats out, you have the right to walk across all the others to reach your own.

When I went to visit the sisters, I had no idea where their junk was in this vast floating city. The Maryknoll missionary who brought me was trying to explain whom we wanted to find, so he used the Chinese word for sister. He inquired after the Little Sisters of Jesus. Everybody knew them and smiled and pointed us in the right direction. After we had been talking to the people for a while, we realized that they thought we were visiting the *flesh and blood family* of our Lord Jesus Christ. These simple peasants had no concept of Christ being on earth two thousand years ago. They thought that his "relatives" were here living in the harbor. It was a strange feeling. Here I was, going to visit the Holy Family!

In the evening, the Buddhist people light little tapers at the stern of their junks where each one has a little shrine. When the sun sets, the whole harbor grows quiet for a moment and they sing a little hymn. The sisters sing a Christian hymn and also light tapers. When they sing the "Salve Regina" in Chinese, there is a hush.

The importance of these sisters' patient witness becomes clear when you realize that the Chinese people are trying to figure out this person Jesus Christ. They don't know who he is. They don't realize he lived a long time ago; some of them don't even know he died, much less rose from the dead. But they are impressed by the fact that Christians come from all over the world and build cathedrals, hospitals, missions, and schools. They perform wonderful acts of kindness in all those big buildings adorned with crosses.

Those who live in such poverty may be thinking, "This Christ must have a lot of money. His followers must be very well off. These American and European Christians, the whole crowd of them, are very wealthy people. But isn't it nice that Jesus' own sisters come to live with us poor people in the harbor?"

They are very impressed by that fact. Isn't that the secret of bringing the gospel to the hungry? In India, you will find many people who could not tell you the name of the president of India, but they would know who Mother Teresa is. Why? Because she believes that some of the followers of Jesus should choose to live among the little people.

◆ ◆ ◆

O Lord Jesus Christ, Savior and Redeemer, show me the real way to be your follower. Give me the wisdom and humility to learn from your words and from the church which you left after raising up disciples in your own time.

By your example and by your Holy Spirit, deliver me from following my own way, from constructing the image of you that suits my own needs and desires. Each of my inner inclinations can seduce me to construct my own image of you: my anger, cupidity, self-indulgence, arrogance, self-justification, and sense of self-importance. Like the apostles, I can have my own ideas of how you can save the world—but with my help, of course.

Break my pride by your humility, unmask my selfishness and innate paganism by your providential gifts that impel me to true conversion and humiliation. If necessary, let the knife cut deeply and let me not cringe back in cowardice. Let me know the true joy of your real presence; let me experience even in the dark time, the saving strength of your cross; let me be a source of your gracious assistance to those whom I meet along the way.

Constantly advance your kingdom within all believers so that we may be in reality less pagan and more truly Christian in what we desire. Call back to yourself the lost sheep and bring us together in your fold which is never lost, but endures to ages without end. Amen.

Sheep among the Wolves

"Behold, I send you out as sheep in the midst of wolves; so be wise as serpents and innocent as doves. Beware of men; for they will deliver you up to councils, and flog you in their synagogues, and you will be dragged before governors and kings for my sake, to bear testimony before them and the Gentiles. When they deliver you up, do not be anxious how you are to speak or what you are to say; for what you are to say will be given to you in that hour; for it is not you who speak, but the Spirit of your Father speaking through you."

Mt 10:16-2/

I HAVE SOME SMALL INKLING of how a sheep feels when rounded by wolves after participating in Operation Res Dobb's Ferry, New York. In this picturesque little town on the banks of the Hudson River, I saw priests and r brothers and sisters manhandled, arrested, put in restraints, and dragged into police vans. My own com brothers stood quietly saying the rosary. Using obscene language, a woman in a black leather outf eral minutes demonstrating the use of condoms on feet from their faces. Some protestors wore sat

symbols. In the midst of the blasphemy and cursing, the police did nothing to stop them.

Probably 99 percent of the people who live in Dobb's Ferry do not agree with such outrageous behavior, regardless of their political position. Many of them do not agree with Operation Rescue either. The purpose of a rescue is to use civil disobedience to underscore the injustice of abortion—the destruction of a human life. Nobody enjoys being thrown into the slammer. But it is a very concrete way to be a witness against paganism.

My painful experience in Dobb's Ferry brought back memories of happier times. I spent my first fourteen years as a priest in this friendly community, as chaplain of the Children's Village, a treatment center for emotionally disturbed children built on the hill above the town. Now I saw my beloved Dobb's Ferry torn apart, humiliated, shamed, corrupted.

On other occasions, members of our little Franciscan community have been accosted while praying at abortuaries. Within the sound of obscene cat calls, the pro-life demonstrators stand with their heads down, quietly praying. The louder the screaming and yelling grows, the more persistently do we pray. Often we are joined by evangelical clergy or Orthodox rabbis. One day the rabbi next to me was hauled away by the police. I was left holding up his end of a big banner which read "Rabbis of New York Protest Abortion."

On one occasion, an abortion clinic voluntarily closed because of the huge number of pro-life demonstrators. When our brothers in their gray habits turned away and proceeded home on the subway, they were followed by a number of pro-abortion demonstrators who thought they were moving on to another clinic. Suddenly these women were terrified to find themselves in the middle of the subway station in a run-down section called Fort Apache. This gave our brothers the first opportunity they had ever had to speak to them. In fact, the brothers remained with the women to see that they got safely back on the subway. One of the protestors admitted that they had listened to the other side for the first time.

I wondered what it was like to be an agnostic until I became a political agnostic. I was born a Democrat and became a Christian two weeks later when my parents had me baptized. As I grew older, I personally affirmed not only my commitment to the Lord but also my membership in the Democratic party.

I never dreamed I would be among those standing outside of the 1992 Democratic National Convention in protest of the immoral position that this party has taken in regard to issues of life. My heart ached to see many delegates going in and out of Madison Square Garden with pro-abortion signs. Here and there, I was encouraged to meet "Democrats for Life" who bravely registered a protest vote in favor of pro-life legislation.

During that week a few pro-life meetings were held in Catholic churches in mid-town Manhattan. I was scheduled to speak at St. Agnes Church next to Grand Central Station on a Wednesday evening. Forty-third Street was filled with screaming pro-abortion picketers. As the police arrived to clear the entrance, many of the women disrobed and paraded themselves in an incredible spectacle of public indecency. To offend the sensibilities of those who had come to pray for the preservation of life, other misguided souls wore diabolical insignias and carried signs blasphemous to God, Christ, and the Blessed Virgin.

The issue of abortion has divided Americans more than any other since slavery during the Civil War. Unfortunately, many who call themselves by the name of Christ fail to recognize the moral responsibility of civil government to protect the lives of all human beings—including the unborn. I am grateful that in this sea of confusion, the Catholic Church has held the line in the fight for life in the United States.

While you may not agree with the rescue approach of civil disobedience and confrontation, what would you do to express your disapproval of the widespread killing of unborn children? Such demonstrations do offer a prime opportunity to think about paganism and our responsibility to protect the helpless and vulnerable. Christians follow someone who holds out the promise of eternal life; unbelievers vainly try to grasp the false promise of this world, even as it slips through their fingers.

Some of those militant pro-abortion demonstrators may have gone home with something to think about as well. Faced with vicious screaming, the rescuers do not respond in kind. Even little old nuns are willing to be arrested and dragged into police vans. Some are then humiliated in prison by being strip-searched among other indignities.

Where does one get the courage to go like a lamb to the sacrifice? Many of those arrested are by nature mild souls. Where did the church itself get the strength to stand against overwhelming military might in the former Soviet Union and in Central America? Where do we get the insight—the light, if you will—to see paganism in our own society, where so many other well-meaning people don't see it? The courage, faith, and insight come to us from the Holy Spirit through the church.

NOT ON OUR OWN

The word disciple means someone who has been taught by someone else. We are taught by Jesus Christ in the Scriptures and by the work of the Holy Spirit in our lives. We are taught through the church. Hopefully, we listen. And then we do not send ourselves, but are, rather, *sent* by divine grace. Those who have the blessing of Baptism are sent by their baptismal promises and sanctifying grace. Those who have the gift of Holy Orders are sent by the apostolic commission given by the imposition of the hands.

None of us has the ability to bring the truth of God or to send ourselves. We are sent with a message, and we are commissioned to pass it on, just as it has been given to us.

Even as disciples of Christ, each of us remains vulnerable to confusion and error. While I was working on this book on Puget Sound, I met an elderly gentleman who obviously enjoyed talking. Well-spoken and informed, he apparently spent a lot of time reading the Bible and praying. Because of his theological convictions, this seemingly devout grandson of a Norwegian Lutheran bishop had quit going to church. Too much squabbling, he said, and proceeded to explain his own theology to me. He is convinced that we human beings are the fallen angels who have been given a chance in this brief life to reclaim our place in heaven. If we don't behave, we go right down the chute to hell. Theologically, this man was way out in left field—actually out of the ball park! He is an example of a disciple on his own. He needed a church to provide clear guidance.

History is filled with earnest disciples who did the wrong thing at the wrong time, sometimes disastrously. Because they forgot to listen to the Lord and struck out on their own, many got into water over their heads. Their intentions may have been good, but their mistaken actions did more harm than good.

To be disciples of Christ, we must be part of a praying community. The distinguished Anglican, Evelyn Underhill, writes that the founders of the world religions either started a prayer community or already belonged to one. Our Lord belonged to one such praying community, that of the Jews. We sometimes forget that Jesus was a Jew to the core. A community, Underhill suggests, keeps disciples on a realistic spiritual road. Our Lord did not need a community, but he realized that his followers did.

Thus our Lord started a new praying community which came to be known as Christianity. Jesus was not a lone ranger. He gathered around himself a small band of twelve apostles, as well as a larger community of disciples. His followers strengthened him in his own daily struggle of obedience to the Father, while at the same time they received from him the spiritual formation to carry on after his crucifixion.

Underhill's explanation of why the believer should belong to a praying community indicates that one should not be satisfied to belong just to a "television church." While the sick and the elderly may deeply benefit from a TV Mass or service, they nonetheless need to belong to a church. If you start to go off the deep end, the church will pull you back. It won't let you get too far into outer space before those in charge threaten to revoke your membership. My ex-Lutheran friend who thought we are all fallen angels provides a perfect example. His reading of the Bible with his own interpretation had gotten him into bizarre speculation beyond the pale of orthodoxy.

I have seen several devout people have the tragic experience of losing their faith because of intriguing but false revelation. While a doctoral student at Columbia University, I was taught by Helen Shuchman, the writer of the so-called Course in Miracles. This very sincere and once-agnostic woman spontaneously wrote a long book of psuedo-mystical revelation, without any plan or decision to do so.

Some of the ideas were very beautiful, some absurd. Some were very much in harmony with the truths of the Gospels, while others were not—although the contradictions were hidden in vague, poetic language. It is a long story which I have told in my book, *A Still Small Voice.*[1] Suffice it to say here that by this course, many have "made shipwreck" of their faith.

Others who were intrigued, however, pulled back. What was the difference? What saved many was their willingness to be guided by the church which has transmitted the Scriptures and taught their authentic interpretation. Without the living voice of Christ speaking through the ages in the church, the proclamation of the truths of salvation would have ceased long ago.

The appropriate response to the call of Christ is discipleship. A believing Christian, no matter what his or her denomination, feels the summons to heed the teaching of the Master. We are all to be channels of his goodness to a deperate and starving world.

How does one become a disciple? And at what point does zeal become fanaticism? When zeal turns destructive, the problem is not the Christian faith, but more likely, an emotional disturbance, or at least, a warped view of life. No denomination has cornered the market on fanatical disciples.

While every Christian is called to be a sincere and committed disciple, none of us can judge how another is called to do that. But we each can ask ourselves, am I a true disciple?

SUFFICIENT EVIDENCE TO CONVICT?

Faith, in the biblical sense, is not simply an intellectual conviction, but a way of life. Someone once asked the question: If there were a persecution and they arrested you for being a Christian, would they find sufficient evidence to convict you?

Being a disciple of Christ is a great privilege. Are you following him as sincerely as you are able? Are you receiving God's grace to love him more fully, one day at a time, in all that you do and say? And the crucial question: Are you following God as he wants you to follow him? Our Lord Jesus Christ did not leave it up to his disciples to determine where and when to follow him. He clearly determined and established his own way, his own church.

The church is a collection of Christ's disciples who are under the guidance of the successors of the apostles, a body of followers to whom the Lord has given personal commands and counsels. As instructed in the Sermon on the Mount, his disciples are not to hold grudges, but to pray for their enemies and love them. They are to avoid lust of the heart and not just the act of adultery. They are not to resort to violence, and are even to pray for those who persecute them.

Christ counsels us to pray always, and to pray and fast in secret. He tells us not to take pride in our virtues, not to serve God in order to be seen, not to worry, not to judge. Instead, we are to visit the sick and the imprisoned, to give clothing to the naked, to comfort the sorrowful, and to do other works of charity and mercy.

We also need to read Scripture regularly to make sure we are staying on track and not forgetting something significant. When I am reading the Scriptures, I often discover that I've forgotten whole clumps of things I'm sometimes supposed to do, things that I'm frequently neglecting. Have you ever had this experience? David lamented, "My sin is always before me."

If we want to be disciples of Christ as he determined and commanded, we must be disciples in the church, members of the body of Christ. God saves us to be part of his very own people, and our salvation cannot be fully understood apart from that reality.

How can we describe the essential elements of the church founded by Christ? There are different ways that one can arrive at the answers to this question, but in the pages ahead I'm going to approach it from what we call the four marks of the church: One, Holy, Catholic, and Apostolic.[2]

TRYING TO KEEP IT TOGETHER—THE ONE CHURCH

That the Catholic Church remains united as one is the sovereign work of the Holy Spirit. Jesus spoke at length to the disciples at the Last Supper about unity (see Jn 14-17). He promised to send the Spirit of truth to give us counsel and unity. We are exhorted to love our brothers and sisters and to remain united with them, even when we disagree with them.

Our Lord could just as well have said, "Wherever two or three are gathered in my name, there will be a squabble." The Acts of the Apostles and the Epistles describe pretty substantial disputes among the followers of Jesus, some pitting one great saint against another.

Did you expect that we were going to do better? It is dangerously utopian and ultimately narcissistic to think that we are going to belong to a praying community or even a family where everyone agrees sweetly on everything. Even our new community of fervent, faith-filled friars has its share of disputes. Some of us are more contemplative, others more active; some are more traditional, others more contemporary—despite our agreement on fundamentals. Mother Angelica, the sage founder of a cloister as well as the Eternal Word Television Network, once told me, "It's all part of the package." Accepting that truth is a big step toward humility.

We should work toward Christian unity because that was the heart of Jesus' prayer at the Last Supper: "I do not pray for these only, but also for those who believe in me through their word, that they may all be one; even as thou, Father, art in me, and I in thee, that they also may be in us, so that the world may believe that thou hast sent me" (Jn 17:20-21). The minute we give in to hate and division, we lessen the impact of our witness as the people of God.

Think of this: Catholics number almost a billion souls— every one of them born with original sin. One billion of any-thing is an awful burden to consider—bottle tops, cancelled postage stamps, rusty nails. And, here the Catholic Church is, the oldest and largest organization in the world, trying to keep a billion sinners together in the midst of a hostile environment!

Most of us who went to parochial school years ago studied the four marks of the church from a kind of triumphalistic per-spective. Where I grew up, the Protestants were elderly folks who behaved well and didn't cuss. These sweet old ladies and gentlemen went to churches that did not seem very popular. The first Protestant clergyman I ever knew was Lutheran. A kindly old man, he lived next door.

In contrast, we younger Catholics did not use such proper language. The Jewish kids were better dressed and had names like Joel and Melvin, while my Catholic buddies went by saintly names such as Anthony, Patrick, and Kevin. The few Protestant kids had funny ones like Woodrow and Warren. The fact that we all got along helped me gain an appreciation for those of other faiths. God loves and seeks us all.

I can't brag about the Catholic Church in this particular con-text. Despite our fractiousness, despite our very worst efforts, the Catholic Church remains remarkably united. On the far right, Archbishop LeFebvre, who died a few years before this writing, clung adamantly to an ultra-traditional Catholicism and refused to incorporate the liturgical changes prescribed by the pope. The group he founded is presently in schism and out of the church.

On the far left, Catholic unity is threatened by members who argue too vehemently for the ordination of women. Others advocate teachings quite contrary to those of the bishops and pope. In Washington, D.C., a black priest started his own

African Catholic Church. He also invalidly ordained a woman. He claims to still be a part of the Catholic Church, even though he is in open rebellion against it.

I am quite sure that today, under Catholic auspices, we can find groups attempting to celebrate the liturgy without a priest. Though such liturgies are completely invalid, these people don't seem to care. Any group can start a schismatic church simply by convincing somebody to ordain them, perhaps a schismatic bishop. While this saddens me, not much surprises me anymore.

In the middle of all this confusion, we have this huge group of nine hundred fifty million sinners plodding along with everybody mad at us. "Why don't you do this?" "Why don't you do that?" Such is the diverse unity of the Catholic Church. How has this very improbable organization managed to hold together against such tremendous odds?

A number of other large Christian churches have, over time, broken into different denominations, as a result of doctrinal differences or even geography. Ever since the Reformation, many of these groups have been splintering into smaller and smaller fragments. In the United States, three different denominations of Quakers have been arguing about how to be silent together. I'm sure they think the issues are all terribly important, and perhaps they are. I just don't understand how such peaceful people could generate serious disagreements over such things.

But don't laugh. We could have exactly the same splintering in the Catholic Church. Except for one reality. The only thing that stops us from disintegrating is not the pope, not the bishops, and not the Baltimore Catechism. It is the *presence of Christ himself* who mysteriously holds the church together by the indwelling of the Holy Spirit. In fact, the Holy Spirit dwells within everyone who is in a relationship of grace with God, no matter what church they belong to. There are also elements of truth and grace in various Christian churches. But God dwells only in one church *in the fullness of grace and truth*—the Catholic Church which Jesus Christ founded.

We Catholics are still in the ship of Peter by reason of the Holy Spirit. That this incredible organization continues to hang together just doesn't make sense from a sociological and historical point of view.

Thomas Babington McCauley, the great British historian who was Protestant, pointed out that the Catholic Church was there when all the governments of the world began and when all the kings were crowned, and has continued to stand while they have all fallen. The church existed long before northern Europe was civilized. McCauley observed that someday a visitor from New Zealand may sit among the ruins of London sketching what is left of St. Paul's Cathedral, and the Catholic Church will still be there.

Why? *Because of the love of Christ which gives the Holy Spirit.* The church is one not because some especially tenacious human beings have decided to stick together no matter what. The Catholic Church is one *only* because Christ is at the heart of it. Jesus is the founder and the head of the church. It stays together because Jesus Christ himself holds it together.

We do not have two Catholic Churches. When people have attempted to start another Catholic Church—whether it be an African American church or a church retaining the Latin Mass—it has become simply another denomination. Sometimes I think we Catholics act like we are just another denomination. We often don't act like we really believe that Christ is at the center of our church, that he is the one responsible for its unity. When we cause disunity, we are in fact attacking Christ himself, as St. Paul believed.

How do you respond to being a member of this extremely diverse group? Where would you place yourself on the spectrum of right to left? Do you support or work against the unity of the church? How often do you pray that Christ would strengthen our leadership and our unity by the outpouring of his grace?

Most importantly, do you love Christ and do you love your brothers and sisters, even when you disagree with them? We certainly have ample room to criticize and disagree, but let us hold fast to the precious gift we have received in the Catholic Church. At the same time, let us be careful to avoid being proud of belonging to the Catholic faith. We belong in spite of ourselves.

CRACKED EARTHENWARE POTS—THE ONE, HOLY CHURCH

Our big claim to fame used to be that the Catholic Church is *holy* because it teaches a holy doctrine and calls people to a holy life. Perhaps you remember that answer from your catechism. But by the same token, couldn't we also say that the Catholic Church is *unholy* because of the eminent *unholiness* of so many of its children?

Indeed, the Catholic Church is holy and unholy at the same time. But the holiness is in one realm and the sinfulness is in another. Simply put, the Catholic Church is a collection of sinners. It is not holy simply because it has many holy people. It also has plenty of not-so-holy people. Rather, it is holy because it was established by Christ to fulfill his mission in the world. Linguistically, "holy" simply means different, transcendent, set apart, beyond the causes and estimation of this world.

Almost in spite of itself, the Catholic Church has been able in the worst of moments to call people to holiness. It continues to call us by unearthly or holy means—namely, through the sacred Scriptures, the sacraments, and the Tradition that has been passed on since the time of Christ. God uses all of these means to touch and heal our wounds.

We have to be careful here. I am not saying that other religious denominations don't call people to holiness or that they don't have holy members. I don't mean that at all. But I am saying that there is some radical, basic, or existential reality at the center of the Catholic Church which, even in the worst of times, can call someone to holiness.

The church does not produce its own holiness, but is the recipient of the holiness which Christ gives it. Individual Catholics themselves may be unholy in the sense that they are not living good Christian lives. In fact, I am often embarrassed about how many Protestants seem to outshine us in love for God and evangelical zeal, as well as love of neighbor and Christian service.

I don't mean to be unjust to other denominations at all. But the Catholic Church itself is holy since it came from God. Christ established the holy Catholic Church. It remains holy even when its members or leaders are unholy. This fact doesn't give us great reasons to be *proud* of being Catholic. It should instead cause us to be *scared silly* because we have so many powerful means to holiness, yet might still be going against the very holiness of the church.

St. John Bosco, who died about a hundred years ago, is supposed to have said that he went to the worst seminary in the world. Yet that one seminary turned out five canonized saints in two generations! Sometimes the worst of moments in church history turns out the most saints. Perhaps it's a matter of purification under fire.

One study discovered that in the century before Martin Luther hung his famous thesis on the cathedral door, at least one person was born every single year who would become a canonized saint. Some of the greatest saints were born in that hundred years—including Teresa of Avila, John of the Cross, and Ignatius Loyola.

The church is holy because the Holy Spirit is in the church— *not the other way around!* We often become discouraged by scandals in the media about clergy. Serious accusations are sometimes made which cannot be substantiated, yet do damage nonetheless because they make such a sensational story. Too often, these accusations have some ground in reality. Even so, how many of us who criticize would slip and fall if we were faced by the same difficult challenges?

In any event, though saddened, we should not be overwhelmed by scandals concerning clergy, even in high places.

The church has survived a lot worse. Not because of human holiness, but the holiness of the church established by Christ. By far the worst scandal in the history of the Catholic Church occurred when Judas Iscariot betrayed Jesus, and all the other apostles, save John, ran away.

How do you respond to the holiness available in the sacraments and Scriptures at the heart of the church? I hear so much bellyaching about the church. In my travels, parishioners tell me that their pastor doesn't preach the gospel, or they feel no sense of community in the parish, or the pastor is always asking for more money, or the music is bad. No matter what we do, we clergy seem to get criticized from some direction.

When Cardinal John O'Connor came to New York, I warned him as a friend of many years about the perils he faced. I said, "Your Eminence, let me tell you something about New York City. It's like a four-masted schooner caught in a hurricane. You as the captain are lashed to a mast with only one arm free, desperately trying to grab random pieces of the cargo as they get washed over the side. New York City has been somewhat out of control since the Civil War. Things probably haven't improved, but they can't get much worse. New York has been described as Babylon and Jerusalem wrapped up together in a hot dog roll!"

But where else should the church be? Except right in the middle of it all! The church needs to be on Fifth Avenue at St. Patrick's Cathedral and in the poorest slums. I am grateful to be down in the South Bronx along with the brothers and sisters of our community. Someone once said to me, "What an awful place to start a religious community!" I answered, "It's marvelous." We are surrounded by other Christians, especially the store-front-chapel variety. There are all kinds of Catholic religious: Franciscan Brothers of San Damiano, Missionaries of Charity, Redemptorists, Sisters of Christian Charity, Mother Seton's Sisters of Charity, Dominicans, Ursulines, Franciscan Friars Minor, along with Augustinian Recollects, with many very dedicated diocesan priests. We have so many religious houses and works that our vicar, Bishop Francisco Garmendia, calls the Bronx "Our Lady's Playground." The newspapers and the police rarely see it that way.

Those who attack the church and expose its wounds for public ridicule seldom talk about the tremendous number of works of charity which go on quietly in the church all over the world, including the Bronx. Why should we stay there? Not because of anything we in our brokenness can bring. We are all nothing but poor sinners, cracked earthenware. From between the cracks, the love of Christ can shine out. We don't personally bring holiness to our neighborhoods. We respond to the presence of God, to the suffering of Christ in the midst of the poor. We are especially privileged to bring the sacraments and the presence of Christ to such bleak places.

As I scan my memory for illustrations of Christ's presence in the world through the church, I feel overwhelmed. Whenever we are willing to let Christ work through us, he does so. Whether it be the incredible works of the Missionaries of Charity in Calcutta, or the quiet embrace of the volunteer mother from the suburbs trying to help a little girl do her lessons, Christ is there.

I think of the free care given by the Hawthorne Dominicans to terminally ill cancer patients who cannot afford treatment, or priests teaching farming techniques to people who live in remote sections of Africa. Sadly, there are never enough of these incredible works because of the decline in religious vocations. "Some of the seed fell among the thorns, where they sprang up and choked it."

In family life, one can find some of the most patient and generous acts of Christian love expressed in the tender care of the elderly and the retarded. I know from counseling and confessions that this care is most often given by those who are trying to follow the example of Christ.

One person who exemplifies the love of Christ shining in the church is a quiet layman who lives in Harlem. I will call him Tony. He was cared for by the Catholic Church from before his birth at the New York Foundling Hospital, then at St. Agnes Orphanage, and lastly at the Pope Pius School. Tony finally went out on his own, but still needed a place to live and a helping hand when he went to college. Then he lived in our St. Francis House for several years while he worked and got his education.

Tony's mother has always suffered from severe mental disorders. Since she was not able to care for herself, Tony has lovingly cared for her since he got out on his own. After working for a brokerage house for an unfair wage and receiving no benefits, he obtained a position in the courts. Tony is probably the most honest and reliable person I have ever met. Every two weeks on payday, he travels to the Bronx to give us a donation, usually fifty dollars, for our work with the poor.

Stories like Tony's are repeated countless times. They reflect the love of Christ for the poor, but they are also examples of love given back by those who have received it.

THE ONE, HOLY, CATHOLIC CHURCH

The church is also *catholic*, meaning that it exists in all ages and extends to all people. Catholic derives from two Greek words, *kata holos*: from out of everything, universal. When our religious community went to the papal audience in Rome, St. Peter's Square was overflowing with the faithful on a radiant, sunshiny day. Our group had been able to get tickets for seats right behind the cardinals. We were excited and expecting something very different. My thought as I waited for my encounter with the Vicar of Christ was, "Good heavens, how does this man put up with all of this? No one should have to put up with what this pope endures!"

The nearly forty thousand people present must have belonged to well over one hundred twenty-five different groups—each of which was formally recognized by name. It was unbelievable! Fuller Brush agents from St. Louis stood up and clapped, and the pope waved to them. The Schnitzel Band from Cincinnati played a few bars and the pope waved to them. But the one that really surprised me was a group of Lutheran Sunday school teachers from Minnesota, who sent up a cheer from their place in the vast expanse of St. Peter's Square. Of course, Pope John Paul gave them a big wave. They even called out our little community's name and we stood up and enthusiastically waved. The pope must genuinely love people. And he knows to the core of his being that the church is catholic.

Standing next to us was the archbishop of Krakow, who had grown up under the Nazis. Next to him were two jet-black young men, cutting very handsome figures in their bishop's robes trimmed with red. They were from Mali in Africa. Next to them were some bishops from Germany.

Then we saw a young man, poorly dressed but with a bishop's cassock under his jacket. He was from a Communist country and had been secretly ordained behind the Iron Curtain. After being surrounded by cheering mobs in St. Peter's Square, he would be returning to a diocese which is a whole country, without a single church building. Next to him were two or three bishops from New South Wales, Australia, and Argentina. Across the way were bishops who had been allowed to come from an Asian Communist country. What a thrilling experience! The incredible mix of laity, religious, and clergy from all over the world was staggering.

Such universality exemplifies what the word "catholic" means. The church did not make this unanimity for itself. It arises from the grace of Christ. In fact, we all need to be careful because we all want to keep someone out. Let's face it—we all have our little prejudices. Even those who are the object of prejudice have targets of their own. But that doesn't fit with the nature of the Catholic Church—whether our prejudice stems from issues of race, national origin, psychological problems, economics, or personal difficulty and struggle. The Catholic Church will always include people that you and I would consider disreputable. In the Good Counsel Homes for unmarried mothers that I mentioned previously, some of the young women come from extremely poor homes; others are documented or undocumented aliens who have come into the city desperate, looking for work, and have had affairs with men. Some are simply young girls from the streets.

The world sometimes calls these young women by nasty names. Yet such women have been cared for by the church for centuries and have had their babies baptized. One such woman, Rosie, came from a poor, almost primitive, family. Her mother was extremely inadequate. Young and naïve, Rosie had an affair with her boyfriend and became pregnant. The baby died before birth, possibly from malnutrition. Because of the emotional upheaval set off in her family, Rosie became alienated from that primitive support group. She saw nowhere else to make a living but in the streets.

Rosie never developed a permanent relationship with anyone. She was so naïve that very quickly she conceived another child and had no place else to go until someone referred her to the Foundling Home. There she was taken care of and developed some self-esteem and perspective on life. Rosie then came to the Good Counsel Homes, where she will be able to get some education and job training while the baby grows. Hopefully, she will be able to share an apartment with another young mother, when both of them have learned enough to take responsibility for their own lives. The cycle of prostitution can be broken only by such labors of love.

Jesus said that he came to save sinners, not the just. He came to heal the sick and not the healthy. St. Benedict Joseph Labré is the patron of homeless people. When you pass one of these poor folks on the street, don't forget that they have their own patron saint who himself was a homeless and mentally ill vagabond for fourteen years. The church's arms are open infinitely wider to the huddled masses than are those of the Statue of Liberty.

Sometimes I wonder how much we Catholics are the obstacles to the catholicism or the universality of the church. Because other churches do not have such ancient and broad roots, they could be forgiven for prejudice and narrowness much more easily. We Catholics have no excuse.

A friend who was an Episcopalian priest has been ordained a Catholic priest with a pastoral provision for married clergy. He told me, "The thing that we notice when we go to the Catholic Church is that everyone is there. It is so mixed up, so heterogeneous." That is exactly the challenge. No one is to be left out. But we Catholics should examine our personal consciences on this score.

Not too many years ago, an African-American Catholic in the South who attended Mass in a "white" church received Communion last—just as black people were expected to ride at the back of the bus. In some areas, I have heard that they even received Communion *after* the liturgy was ended. Granted, many whites thought such a practice was ridiculous and wanted it stopped, but it is an example of prejudice embedded right in the heart of the church, a prejudice which is absolutely unacceptable.

Sometimes it's helpful to be part of a minority. Once when I walked through Nairobi, Kenya, I didn't see another Caucasian for several blocks. I began to know what it felt like to be in a minority. The first "white" person I saw was an albino girl, who was actually a native of Kenya. I expected her to speak to me in English, but of course, she couldn't.

A speaker at the annual meeting of the interracial forum in New York City was an African American, the district attorney of the Bronx and a graduate of St. Paul's School. We talked about how much good has been accomplished in interracial relations, but how much progress remains to be made. He reminded me that even a successful person like himself can encounter subtle forms of prejudice.

I know a young seminarian who has suffered a great deal in the process of converting from Judaism. His family does not understand; it is a very bitter pill for them to swallow. I can certainly sympathize with their consternation and he himself showed great understanding. However, every once in a while he still hears an anti-Semitic remark from his fellow Catholics. I said to him, "That's the price of belonging to the largest and most heterogeneous organization in the world. We have all kinds of schleps!"

Such prejudice is most unfortunate, but a good deal of improvement has taken place in my lifetime. Not so long ago, an Irish-Italian wedding was considered a mixed marriage; the ecumenical movement meant the Poles were speaking to the Hungarians! My Alsatian grandfather was snubbed for marrying an Irish girl. She had never seen Ireland and he had never seen Alsace-Lorraine.

Since the victims of prejudice often carry deep-seated wounds for life, some efforts to combat prejudice can backfire. Don't be surprised if you are the recipient of resentment and prejudice that you never held or had given up years ago. I sometimes experience prejudice against white people while working with the poor. By accepting it as penance for my own sins, I manage to get a little bit ahead in the battle against my own vices.

I never considered myself a male chauvinist pig or even a male chauvinist mosquito. I grew up in a family where the boys were taught to respect women. You held doors, you stood up when a lady came into the room, you walked next to the curb, and you watched your language. This tradition continued on smoothly into the Capuchin seminary.

Like many priests, I had women bosses, nuns, and social workers. I got told off when I needed it and even when I didn't deserve it. I accepted it from women as I did from men. It never dawned on me that this gentlemanly courtesy could be construed as a form of control. I never wanted to control anybody. I just wanted to get the job done because eternity will come all too soon. I have a special liking for strong, efficient women. Can you imagine trying to talk Mother Teresa or Mother Angelica into something? I've tried.

I never thought I had the upper hand because I was a man. I never even thought I had the upper hand at all. One thing I will admit to: I do find women a bit mysterious. I admire a special feminine intuition about people and things, and although a fairly intuitive man, I am frequently outclassed. If this is a prejudice, I confess.

It seems to me that the new cultural role of women is an inevitable part of the same complex processes that affect all human beings moving toward a one-world society. The cultural identity of women is changing, right along with the cultural identity of men. We are all in this together. Some people like to blame the subjugation of women on Christianity or the Judeo-Christian tradition. They ought to travel outside the Western world; they would quickly see that the role of women has changed far more quickly where Christian values have dominated. Some people would like to blame the church for the position of women and everything else that has gone wrong. That is prejudice, too.

I recently read an article by a female anthropologist about a group of Tibetan nuns whose order had existed for a thousand years. These nuns had complained to the author that they were dominated by the monks. Maybe they had some good reason for complaint. I could certainly find no evidence in the article of the monks ever taking orders from Tibetan women religious. In comparison, I took orders happily for years from women. And today, in one of my jobs, I report to a religious sister who seems to have it all much more together than most men do.

I am appalled and shocked when women tell me what they have suffered at the hands of some men. I think women, in general, have a very legitimate gripe, as do other victims of prejudice and ill will. But I think I also have a gripe when I get blamed for simply being a man—something I had nothing to do with. I neither determined my own gender, nor established the customs or social attitudes I learned. Nor am I even prepared to defend all of them now. I still like to stand up when ladies come into the room, but I'm getting too old and creaky to get up and down so frequently any more.

What about the Catholic Church in all of this? In defense, let's recall that most of us grew up with a picture of the most important, holy, kindly, magnificent creature as a woman. Mary had it all: virgin, mother, blue-collar housewife, widow, sort of a nun, protectress, and queen. She apparently bossed the Son of God around, which nobody else ever did, except St. Joseph. Don't try to tell anyone like me, who has said at least a million Hail Marys, that the Catholic Church has put women in the back seat.

How about the ordination of women? When the great social prophet Archbishop Helder Camara of Brazil was asked this question, I heard him answer: "I always think with the church." So do I. If the restriction of the Catholic priesthood to men were ever to change, it would most probably require the decision of an ecumenical council. Such a decision would represent the beliefs of the Bishop of Rome, along with the vast majority of Catholic bishops, that this change was in keeping with Scripture and Tradition.

The question is not do I think the ordination of women would be nice or fair or just. Really for me, the only question is, is it possible? The Catholic Church did not establish itself. It is not a movement of people who simply want to be better Christians. The Catholic Church did not establish its own sacraments, but believes that they come from Christ, both scripturally and by the guidance of the Holy Spirit in the Tradition and life of the early church. Jesus conferred his authority on the apostles, and neither he nor the early church ordained priests other than men.

I once attended the ordination of a woman minister in a Calvinist church. I had no problem with this at all. She was a friend and coworker who had been chosen by that church and ordained by that congregation to be a minister. Neither she nor they nor I thought that she was becoming a priest. No problem. I can understand why anyone, including women, want to share in the sacramental priesthood of Christ. I have been a priest for over thirty years and have cherished and loved every day, every sacrament, and every blessing. I'd have to be kind of stupid if I could not imagine that a Christian woman would like to share in this vocation. Yet I have many friends who are men in religious life who never felt called to be priests.

The great pioneer in the teaching of pastoral counseling, Brother John Mark Egan, C.F.C., had a perfect response to anyone who asked him, "Why didn't you go all the way and become a priest?" He would very kindly respond by saying, "Why, if I became a priest, I couldn't be a brother." Not every good Christian needs to be a priest or should become a priest. St. Thérèse of Lisieux said that she would like to have been a priest, but she accepted the impossibility. I have taken care of a lot of other people's kids and would like to have been the father of some of my own. But God spared them and gave them someone else.

Many people of both sexes would like to see the Catholic Church ordain women. Being a limited pragmatist with a practical sense of things, I am sorry to see the priesthood missing out on all this talent. But who am I to argue with God? People on all sides of this issue—those passionately devoted to an all-male priesthood, those who hope for a male and female priesthood, even those who are only willing to accept an all-female priesthood—seem to me to be arguing with God. If they are not arguing with his will, they seem to me to be at least arguing with God's time table.

The Catholic Church is by far the most genuinely universal organization in the world, one which includes people of every cultural group and every style of cultural development and decline. It tries to make room for some fairly radical theologians, right alongside little ladies in African tribes who have lived celibately with their polygamous former husbands. To refuse to work intellectually toward the growth and development of the church can be a sin of sloth or self-indulgence of one's own pet ideas.

On the other hand, to irresponsibly disturb the peace of the church while pushing one's pet ideas can be a sin against charity, justice, and even a presumptuous disrespect for the will of God. We Catholics must be prepared to ask ourselves this question: What will I do if God's apparent will for the church does not agree with my own ideas and my prejudices? The answer to that question will indicate how authentically we are members of the church.

We need to guard ourselves against harboring deep-seated prejudices against others. We each need to pray for the grace to embrace the endless diversity of the universal church. I don't know whether the United Nations will endure—I hope so. But if it doesn't, there will always be the holy Catholic Church.

THE ONE, HOLY, CATHOLIC, AND APOSTOLIC CHURCH

I am constantly amazed how misunderstood the Catholic Church is, even among its own people. Many are not even sure what *apostolic succession* means, perhaps because it's not often discussed. The Catholic Church has a very clear teaching on this subject, while most other churches do not. An apostolic church is one founded by Christ on the apostles and handed down by apostolic succession through the Sacrament of Holy Orders.

The power of Holy Orders and with it, the pastoral responsibility for the faithful, has been handed on by the imposition of hands since the founding of the church. The analogy of the pastor or shepherd was our Lord's own idea. Simply put, every Catholic priest can trace his Holy Orders back to a bishop who eventually goes back to the apostles. For example, I was ordained by Bishop James Griffiths, an auxiliary bishop of New York. He was ordained by Cardinal Spellman, who was ordained by Pope Pius XII. Once you get back to a pope, it's easy to assume that you're in the line that goes all the way back to apostolic times.

For apostolic succession to be handed on by Holy Orders, you only need to have a validly ordained bishop who follows the very simple requirements of the liturgy of ordination with the right intention. For this reason, the Catholic Church recognizes the validity of orders of the Eastern Orthodox Churches.

It is said that one could also make a case for the validity of the orders of some of the Scandinavian Lutheran Churches which always had bishops, beginning with the pre-Reformation Catholic bishops. Sometimes in other churches, as in the Anglican Communion, clergy who were concerned for the validity of their line of orders had themselves conditionally ordained by orthodox bishops.

The Catholic Church also would recognize but not allow people to use ordination obtained illegitimately from little, fly-by-night churches which may have valid orders. Most of these so-called churches have few or no members. If a Catholic were to be ordained without the jurisdiction of a bishop empowered to do so—like a diocesan bishop or a delegated auxiliary—he would be excommunicated even though he would become a priest.

When Archbishop Lefebvre ordained three bishops before his death, the decree of excommunication was formally issued while the liturgy was still going on. Actually the excommunication was automatic with the three illegitimate ordinations. These priests had, of course, been warned not to do this, but they went ahead anyway. Nonetheless, those three men are still ordained bishops of what is, sadly, a schismatic church.

Some Orthodox churches do not believe that Holy Orders can be passed on outside of their church. For example, if a Catholic priest were to become a member of the Russian Orthodox Church—sometimes called the Synod—he would not be accepted as a priest by that group. In fact, he would have to be confirmed and then reordained. The Catholic Church believes that Holy Orders are given *for the people*, rather than for the priest or the bishop. To protect the people from losing the sacraments because of invalidly ordained men, Holy Orders are extended as far as possible. We Catholics are not usually given credit for being so concerned about other people. In fact, the Catholic Church recognizes the validity of Baptism in any church when it is properly performed with the correct intention.

You may ask, "What has all this got to do with my spiritual life? It just sounds like legalistic infighting to me." Five of the sacraments hinge on the validity of apostolic succession: Holy Orders, the Holy Eucharist, the Anointing of the Sick, Confirmation, and that very important one, the Sacrament of Reconciliation (confession). Baptism and Marriage are the only two that can be performed without a priest if necessary. A couple can marry themselves when no priest is available to witness the marriage for a long time. Anyone can perform Baptism. This is how the lay people who had no priests kept the Catholic Church in the Orient alive during centuries of persecution.

We should see apostolic succession as a very cherished gift. How easily we come to the altar to receive the Eucharist! We come into the church to visit the presence of Christ himself in the Blessed Sacrament. We send for a priest when we are dying; we have Confirmation as we grow out of childhood; we go to confession and receive sacramental absolution. All of these precious gifts we take for granted depend entirely on apostolic succession.

St. Margaret Clitherowe, a housewife who lived during the reign of Queen Elizabeth I, endured hideous suffering and death to defend her belief in apostolic succession. The judges asked this woman if she would promise not to hide priests again. Margaret picked up her Bible and told them, "I promise you I *will* hide priests again because they alone bring us the Body of Christ." She was pressed to death on St. Michael's bridge in York over four hundred years ago. A brave woman, indeed, who is now one of the great saints of Catholic history in England.

THOSE WHO HAVE RECEIVED MUCH

Those who should be the most grateful for these sacramental gifts are those who receive Holy Orders. I am always saddened to hear a priest complaining about what a hard life he leads. Surely it can be difficult. Priests can get miserable assignments. I know many who suffer intensely. But a priest once said, "No matter what else happens in a single day, if I offer the Mass well, it has been a perfect day." As I grow older and the meaning of the Holy Eucharist and the Mass becomes clearer to me, I am filled with fear and trembling every time I participate in the sacrifice of Christ in his eternal worship as High Priest of all creation. I wonder sometimes if I will always have enough courage to offer the Mass. The responsibility is so far beyond me that I feel completely unworthy.

Again, the apostolic mark of the church does not depend on our own holiness. The church is made up of human beings just like you and me. The first apostles failed Christ often, even on the night of his arrest. But these same apostles were still entrusted with the mysteries of salvation. And these precious means of salvation are not given to us to do with whatever we like.

Does this teaching of apostolic succession mean that we disparage other churches? By no means. I have a great deal of respect for those who follow Christ according to other traditions. I remember visiting a lady who was sick in the hospital. She belonged to a storefront black church in the Bronx. She said to me, "Now that the white folks are moving out, we're buying all those big churches. I don't want our congregation to buy one because I love my little storefront church. It's just filled with love!"

I answered, "Dear, I'm going to be right down and join up. I never belonged to a parish that was filled with love. I'd be the first member of the Apostolic Church of God in Christ who had the apostolic succession. I'll just have to belong to both churches!"

What does our divine Savior say? "Where two or three are gathered in my name, there am I." Of course, Christ is present in the little church near us in the Bronx named The Little Widow's Mite Church. Of course he is present in the Calvary Baptist Church and the First Presbyterian Church. Where two or three are gathered in his name, Jesus is there.

Through no fault of their own, the people in those churches are not able to partake of the Eucharist. They don't believe that their communion bread is the Body of Christ but only a symbol. Those of other churches can lift up their hearts to the Lord and he certainly hears their prayers and comes to them. Yet in the liturgy, Catholics and Orthodox Christians are privileged to participate in existentially and substantially the same eucharistic feast as the saints in heaven. The Catholic Church teaches that there is only one priest, only one sacrifice, only one Eucharist—Christ.

About one out of every ten thousand people in the world is a Catholic priest. How do you think that makes me feel? Overwhelmingly humbled. About one out of every five people is a Catholic. I can almost see the huge crowd on Judgment Day. I can imagine St. Peter saying, "Step right up here, Benedict, because you received many more blessings than most people. Now, what did you do with all you got?" Frankly, I would rather be a flop at trying to serve our Lord than a success at anything else in the world.

Why does Jesus come to us in the Eucharist? Not because of the priest. Why do we get absolved from our sins? Good heavens, no priest could ever do that for you! How am I able to prepare anyone for death through the Holy Anointing? Only because Christ acts through the apostolic succession in the priest—just as he acts through sanctifying grace in all believers.

Yet all Catholics and all Christians are called to be apostolic, each in his or her own way. We all function at times in the place of Christ. If you do good deeds, they are *his* good deeds, not yours. If we do anything worthwhile or helpful to others, it is Christ who has done them through us. We all share in the apostolic work of Christ, although not in a sacramental sense.

If you feel like an ordinary, everyday Catholic, do not underestimate your position. You may not feel able to do anything apostolic in a sacramental sense, but you certainly can be a witness in your own life, at home, where you work, or where you relax. You can volunteer to teach religious education in your parish and work hard at preparing lessons and teaching children and teenagers the truths of their faith. You can take a stand against pornography and urge people not to patronize places that insist on selling it. You can work at a soup kitchen or deliver meals to the aged at home. You could volunteer to be a eucharistic minister, especially for the sick.

St. Paul constantly reminds us of the many different functions of the church, just as there are many functions in the human body (see 1 Cor 12). Whatever your particular function may be, be faithful and faith-filled. We don't know what Christ may call any of us to do tomorrow. I may have a stroke tomorrow and be incapacitated. I may never preach again. None of us knows the road ahead. The Lord is gracious enough not to burden us with the details of the future—be they ghastly or glorious.

In addition to your other good works, please remember to pray for us priests. Pray for your bishop. Pray for the pope. An old Italian proverb about the pope reads, "Heavy hangs the great mantle on him who would keep it from the mire." The great mantle is the cape of the pope. Heavy hangs that burden on the man who would carry it faithfully and prayerfully and worthily of Christ.

How sad that more Catholics do not respond in the depths of their hearts to the great privilege, the honor, the unimaginable responsibility of belonging to the One, Holy, Catholic, and Apostolic Church. In our own spiritual lives, may we try to be fervent disciples of Christ—right alongside our Orthodox and Protestant brethren—and fervent disciples of God alongside the Jews and the Moslems and the Hindus and the Buddhists. But most of all, let us try to be faithful disciples of Christ in the Catholic Church which he has given to the world.

Despite scandals in society and even the church, many (including some Protestant theologians) say that this is the time for the Catholic Church to manifest itself as the unique vehicle of Christ in the world. Whether or not it lives up to its call depends on the free will of the people who make up the church. It depends on you and me. God acts through us, but God does not force us.

SHARING THE SUFFERINGS OF CHRIST

St. Peter—my favorite, poor, bungling, frightened, converted, yet persistent apostle—has some encouraging words for us in this regard. "Beloved, do not be surprised at the fiery ordeal which comes upon you to prove you, as though something strange were happening to you. But rejoice in so far as you share Christ's sufferings, that you may also rejoice and be glad when his glory is revealed" (1 Pt 4:12-13).

Once upon a time, when we Catholics heard about sufferings of brothers and sisters in other countries, we thought that would never come to us in the United States. However, things may be getting tougher for us in the very near future. The opposition of the church to abortion and euthanasia is going to attract persistent hostility. The employment of some may be affected. Some have already suffered in their political careers. The governor of Pennsylvania was prevented from speaking at the convention of his own party because of his refusal to go along with its pro-death stand. More and more Catholics are going to suffer similar hardships.

Religion in general and the Catholic Church in particular are in for a rough ride these days. We live in difficult times for the church as a whole and for individual Catholics who are willing to stand by the church. For the first time in years the executive branch of the government of the United States has embarked on policies which the Catholic Church condemns as violations of the human right to life. I'm thinking, of course, of President Bill Clinton's policies on abortion. In the wealthy nations of the West, the church is under tremendous attack and pressure in the media. At the same time, Eastern Europe and Russia are coming out of the bondage of Communism. While the media in the United States drags the church and religion through the mud, leaders in Russia, Poland, and Eastern Europe are for the first time in decades presenting religious news in a positive and even complimentary way.

We might sometimes be better off reading news reports from Moscow than New York City! Amazing, isn't it? When a

Havana newspaper took a shot at the Catholic Church, the atheistic government publicly apologized to the Holy See for an attack on the pope. Even though they openly repress the church, they wouldn't dream of doing what is done in our own country every day.

We live in a time when people are critical of everyone—priests, bishops, ministers, rabbis, as well as the pope. I believe Pope John Paul II is a great pope. Because of the attack on his life in St. Peter's Square, he is already in some sense a martyr. He has taken the Catholic Church through most difficult times. He has enemies on all sides. Even though he is a man of awesome natural abilities and talents, he is criticized incessantly. Some clergy and religious are so blinded by their prejudice as to call him stupid and narrow-minded.

I think history will pass a very positive judgment on the man who tore the first hole in the Iron Curtain. Many of the events unfolding in Europe today are the fruit of the groundwork laid a decade ago when Pope John Paul II supported the Solidarity movement in Poland. He is great because he gives all that he has: his life, his time, his energy. He has already made over seventy apostolic journeys. He endangers his life daily by giving audiences to thousands of people.

For the first time in many years, American Catholics have a chance to suffer for the Lord. I have already mentioned those who have gone to jail for the right of babies to live. The point of this civil disobedience is to make people aware of the seriousness and moral tragedy of abortion. I remember a rescue run mostly by women in Englewood, New Jersey. The police called from the surrounding towns looked embarrassed. The mayor of Englewood held a billy club while he directed the arrest of this "dangerous" group of nuns and grandmothers. Shades of Jackson, Mississippi, in the sixties.

I must say, some of the sisters made me proud. If you ever want to see an absurd scene, it's four policemen trying to pick up a nun who is kneeling in the middle of the sidewalk saying her rosary. Incredible! I kept thinking, "Is this the United States of America?"

The first woman who entered the clinic was a teenage girl who looked confused, frightened, and pitiful. A victorious roar of delight went up from the pro-abortion contingent. At the prospect of killing an innocent baby! Within minutes, the child within that girl's womb would be dead. It wasn't a polliwog; it wasn't a bacteria; it was a human being.

How is Christ calling you to defend his little ones? To bear witness for the church? Pray for wisdom and courage in the face of opposition and even persecution, that you may be able to stand up for the cause of Christ. This is the hour of the Catholic Church. May we stand, in solidarity with our brothers and sisters of every denomination who believe in God and his sovereignty! Following Christ is the only safe place to be, no matter what the cost.

◆ ◆ ◆

Holy Spirit, you live in the heart of the church. Without your action, the church, indeed the human race itself would perish. As you did in the earliest dawn of creation and of human life, you pass over the world today and renew the face of the earth. Yet you, Spirit of Life and Love, force no one. You compel no one. You do not intrude. We wait for your coming like the apostles and disciples, in fear and trembling at what is going on around us.

O Holy Spirit, come upon us now in this difficult and dark time. Open hearts and minds to your truth. Strengthen our wills to resist evil and to do good. Give us eyes to see your presence everywhere, even where evil seems to triumph. Heal our wounds and undo the effects of our sinfulness. Then your church, your temple of living stones, will be seen as a safe refuge in the storms that break over the world. Amen.

SIX

Growing in Holiness

Count it all joy, my brethren, when you meet various tri-
als, for you know that the testing of your faith produces
steadfastness. And let steadfastness have its full effect,
that you may be perfect and complete, lacking in nothing.

Jas 1:2-4

How can each of us keep trudging down the sometimes discouraging road that leads to the knowledge and love of God? How can we persist in responding to the movement of God's grace in our individual lives? How easily we become forgetful on our long journey toward God! Hearing how God has broken into the heart and mind of a person who has stumbled onto the wrong path can help us avoid becoming as dry and stale as week-old bread.

I met a certain man through the inspiring movement called Courage, a group of Catholic men and women with a homosexual orientation who strive to lead lives of chastity. He now works as a volunteer in an AIDS hospice and encourages others to join Courage. Some people may not feel completely comfortable with his report of an alleged series of apparitions as the means to his conversion. In any case, few can read his account, which follows, without being moved by the power of God's call in the life of a very ordinary human being—a waiter. Yet when grace comes into an ordinary life, that life becomes extraordinary.

How vividly I remember my utter confusion as an introverted sixteen-year-old boy, too shy to speak about misdirected emotions. Why was I plagued by sexual temptations toward members of my own sex? Rather than reveal my very humiliating dilemma to someone who could help me, I listened to all the schoolyard conversations about queer bars and sexual activity. I began to believe that I was a "queer."

My own passions maturing during the sexual revolution of the sixties, I joined right in with my own confusions, anxieties, frustrations, and fears. I felt more secure with those who shared a similar sexual orientation and found my first gay bar. My initial homosexual experience nauseated me. The purely physical act without any love left me feeling only disgust with the other fellow and myself.

I didn't know enough about God or the church to know that I wasn't doing what he wanted. I intuitively felt my homosexual activity was wrong and wanted to quit, but believed I was obliged to accept my fate. I hated who I was, but in order to live a lie, I fought against that person who I was truly called to be. Continually fed by my arrogant friends, I condemned myself to follow the advice of my own ignorance.

The homosexual world offered nothing but a life of the senses. "If it feels good, do it." I was exposed to a variety of sexual practices, with each different partner acting out a particular fantasy. Masking the insecurity of constantly being used and using, of going from one loveless relationship to another, required masses of alcohol and recreational drugs.

I began to walk the tightrope of a double life: a heterosexual with my relatives and a homosexual with my peers. I gradually became lost in the gay culture—one that offered me only a life of self-indulgence, loneliness, alcoholism, drug addiction, disease, and death. Every day became a search for that special person who could finally satisfy my hunger for true love. I was a slave to passions that were out of control, a morality that was nonexistent, and a love that was only spelled L-U-S-T.

I am one of the fortunate ones though. I did find the love that would end all loves, but not until I was forty years old. His name is renowned for freeing people from blindness, possessions, addictions, diseases, hatred, loneliness, and self-loathing. His name is Jesus, and his mother introduced me to him, but that would not come to pass until I had descended even deeper into my self-made prison, looking for the key that could set me free.

College only made me more miserable. I was lying to everyone, but mostly family and friends who knew nothing of my gay side. When the deceit began to destroy even the few decent relationships I hoped to keep, I left school to get a job. The predominately gay food-service industry seemed a natural fit, first in hotels and later in restaurants.

I was in glory. Since most of my co-workers were gay, I began to come out of the closet even more. My work permitted me to travel. I moved to various cities exploring the gay culture and making more friends, but all the while sensing how pitiful everything was. Drugs and alcohol more and more served to mask my emptiness. The bar scene became an endless round of parties—always searching, hoping that the next person would be the end of the painful search.

As the years passed, I became habituated to my homosexual way of life, feeling contempt for society, but in reality, mostly for myself. I finally settled back in my home city and worked in a major restaurant doing what I do best. I thought little about God, and if I did, it wasn't the true God. I didn't know him at all.

I remember watching television one day, and thinking that if I died right then and there, I would stand before Jesus Christ. He would ask me, "How have you loved?" and I would have to say, "I didn't. I didn't know how!" An eternity of endless horror would begin. I thought about doing volunteer work, but living a self-indulgent life hadn't exactly prepared me for putting myself out for someone else. I felt so painfully trapped.

I look back on those moments now as moments of grace when

God was beginning to get through to me, to help me to turn my life around. My aging body coupled with the ravages of drugs and alcohol at least helped to slow down my bar-hopping and sexual activity. I was getting so tired of it all, the endless tossing to and fro of the gay life. Though still far from salvation, I was finally on the road to freedom, even though I didn't know it yet.

One day I went to work as usual, still quite the hateful person, still doing drugs, drinking on the job, still living a self-indulgent life, but at least more in tune with my age of thirty-nine. The restaurant was fairly slow that day and I was looking forward to getting off early, but the Blessed Mother had other plans. One of the owner's wives was hostessing a luncheon for thirteen ladies. As it turned out, all of these women had been to a place called Medugorje, most several times.

As one of the senior waiters, I was elected to serve the party—much to my disappointment. As the luncheon progressed, I began to hear snippets of conversations, including words like Blessed Mother, Medugorje, apparitions, messages, and secrets. My interest was piqued, but with constantly going in and out of the room, I couldn't catch the full meaning. When the owner finally came in to greet the guests, I told myself that no one was getting another morsel of food until I understood all these references to Mary.

I cornered the owner on his way out and asked him what this Medugorje was all about. Surprised that I had never heard of it, he proceeded to tell me about the reported apparitions of the Blessed Mother in Croatia. He told me about Mary's message of conversion, fasting, renunciation of alcohol, drugs, and all forms of behavior that were against God's law and those of the church, as well as praying the rosary daily and praying for three or four hours a day.

All the while, my heart was going wild with hope. I remember saying to myself, "It's all true! The church has been teaching the truth." None of what Our Lady said disturbed me. Instead I realized that she was showing me the way out of the hell that I had gotten myself into. After work I visited the gift shop at the

*nearby cathedral and bought a rosary and a prayer book. I
began praying in the sanctuary every day, even using my watch
to make sure I didn't cheat the Blessed Mother of her three hours.*

*The first day, I felt very disappointed that no priest manned
the confessional before Mass. I told the Lord that if I couldn't go
to confession, then I couldn't stay for the Mass. That would be
too much for me. When the same thing happened the next day, I
complained to the Lord, "It just isn't fair. You got me here, and
now I can't stay for Mass again. You say you came for sinners.
Well, I'm one of the worst, so why can't I go to confession?"*

*The third day, I ran to the cathedral after work to do my
three hours of prayer. Mass was scheduled for six o'clock with
confessions beforehand, so I thought everything was going to
work out great. But when I arrived at the rectory to receive the
Sacrament of Reconciliation face-to-face, I discovered that no
one would be available before Mass after all, due to an emergency. Determined to go to Communion that day, I pondered
where else I could go for confession. When the parish where I was
raised came to mind, I jumped into my car and drove out
there. I walked right into the confessional and was reestablished
in grace after leaving the church over twenty-three years earlier.*

*That day, our Blessed Mother's prayers were answered. I
finally looked squarely at the homosexual lifestyle that threatened to destroy me and said, "It is finished." Party friends, gay
bars, drugs, alcohol, pornographic books—all of it had to go,
and go it all did. Anyone who was not interested in helping me
to return to the church could no longer be part of my life.*

*The pain of separation was acute, but I believed, prayed,
and persevered, and was rewarded with a growing measure of
freedom. Since that visitation of God's grace in January, 1987,
I have attended Mass, recited fifteen decades of the rosary, and
spent about two hours in adoration of the Blessed Sacrament
every day. After five years of daily prayer in his presence, I know
Jesus is there and alive in the Tabernacle.*

*One night about two to three weeks after my initial conver-
sion as I was meditating on the life of Jesus, I experienced what*

some people call being baptized in the Holy Spirit. Call it what you will, that night I believe that I met the Lord of Lords, the King of Kings, my Savior. I didn't see anything with my eyes, but I felt that I saw him with my soul. It was as if my empty heart was being filled with life, with grace, after so many years of being dead. The Lord taught me what true love is: a commitment to the truth rather than a passing feeling.

The organization, Courage, has been God's gift to me, a means to repay in some small way my own freedom. The Lord always uses our own sinful experiences as a way to help those stuck in the same ruts to find salvation. Even while my flesh had been acting out a homosexual lifestyle, my heart had been screaming for freedom. I know many others who still suffer that same slavery. Without knowing how to be free, they are condemned to continue living a life that they hate. My own prayer of praise has been, "Free at last, thank God Almighty, I'm free at last."

The essential work of our lives is to cooperate with God in restoring the divine image in our being. The goal that we must have in all that we do is to return to him from whom we have come. This process of becoming holy is called *sanctification.* Why is it that thinking about sanctification often provokes guilt, fear, and self-rejection? I myself don't even like this word, which so easily leaves me daunted. Let's look honestly and humbly to see what makes the goal of holiness so intimidating.

CLEARING OUT THE RUBBLE

Sanctification can be compared to remodeling an old house. Suppose you bought a dilapidated one, commonly called a "handy-man special." If you were handy with tools, you might visit the lumber yard and hardware store and buy the necessary materials. You would come up with a plan—perhaps after consulting with an architect and interior decorator—and check your finances to make sure you had the money to complete the project. If you're all thumbs like me, you'd likely hire a professional to do the job.

Have you ever lived in a place that was being remodelled? It's a test of faith, let me tell you. It gets a lot worse before it gets better! Sawdust, the smell of mildew, dirt, and cobwebs are everywhere. Rotted lumber, ancient ceiling and floor tiles, old plumbing fixtures—the pile of junk grows higher and higher. You want to move out because of the chaos, but you keep telling yourself that it's going to be worth it when the job is done. You think order will never be restored. You wonder if you should have started the project in the first place.

Almost inevitably, "cans of worms" are opened that you failed to foresee. As it turns out, the basement floor tiles were made with asbestos, which makes removing them an environmental hassle. Then under the tiles you discover mold and mildew which needs to be killed. Before the carpet goes in, some outdoor concrete work seems to be the only way to eliminate a couple of leaks in the cracked outer walls. On and on it goes, as the bills quickly stack up.

Then slowly, the job starts coming together. You see progress as a fresh coat of paint and wallpaper make the place look like new; plush carpeting covers the old floors; new plumbing and electrical fixtures are installed. Of course, your contractor keeps holding out his hand for more money—but, you think it's worth it. Or at least you hope it will be.

The process of sanctification is like restoring an old house. When we first invite God to move into our hearts, he can find an awful mess. A ton of rot and rubble usually has to be torn out before the new material can be installed. Remember the parable about putting new wine into old wineskins (Lk 5:36-39)? Or our Lord's pointed accusation to the Pharisees about being white-washed tombs (Mt 23:27-28)? Not impressed by their hypocritical show of holiness, Jesus clearly saw the sin hidden in their hearts.

Holiness is not merely the restoration of the divine image on our own—as if we were able to take that on as some sort of do-it-yourself project. Rather, holiness means daily surrendering to God, so that through the grace of the Holy Spirit the divine image may be restored by him. *God restores the image.* Sanctification and holiness are his gifts alone, but he will not give them to us unless we are willing to receive them.

Holiness comes to us through our adoption as children of God in Christ Jesus our Lord. St. Paul describes this process by telling about Moses when he came down from Mount Sinai. His face was shining with the glory of God, so radiant that the people were afraid to look at him. Moses needed to cover himself with a veil until the glory gradually diminished. Paul goes on to tell the Corinthians that through Christ, the veil is taken away from God's face. As his adopted sons and daughters, we are able to come closer to God, into his very presence.

> Such is the confidence that we have through Christ toward God. Not that we are sufficient of ourselves to claim anything as coming from us; our sufficiency is from God, who has qualified us to be ministers of a new covenant, not in a written code but in the Spirit; for the written code kills, but the Spirit gives life.
>
> Now if the dispensation of death, carved in letters on stone, came with such splendour that the Israelites could not look at Moses' face because of its brightness, fading as this was, will not the dispensation of the Spirit be attended with greater splendour? ... And we all, with unveiled face, beholding the glory of the Lord, are being changed into his likeness from one degree of glory to another; for this comes from the Lord who is the Spirit. 2 Cor 3:4-18

What do you think when you hear those words? You know what I think? Good heavens! Good Lord! Reflecting on my spiritual struggles can leave me feeling more depressed than elated. Rather than going from one degree of glory to another, I often feel like I'm dilly-dallying along the way, taking one step forward and two steps backward. Progress seems slow and painful, sometimes imperceptible. My most common feeling is that I'm sliding down the slippery slope of sin rather than soaring into the heights of glory. The more I pray, the more I try, the worse my walk with the Lord sometimes seems to get.

When I was a young fellow, I thought that holiness was just around the corner. One New Year's Day I went to see the Capuchins in Brooklyn. The vocations director was explaining the schedule, saying that every day at noon they stopped to examine their consciences to see what sins they had committed. I looked at those old souls and wondered what possible sins could they have!

Well, I found out: the same ones I have! I remember the priest encouraging me with the words, "Don't worry, you'll have something to work on." And indeed I did. More than enough for one lifetime, without a doubt.

WHAT IS A SAINT?

A saint is someone who goes through this restoration without grumbling and complaining, completely surrendered to the process of sanctification. They have not settled for cosmetic improvement, but have sought cleansing and healing of their original wound from the inside out.

Referring to the whole world as a "saint-making machine," Peter Kreeft writes that our fundamental vocation in life is to be saints. Did you think such a calling was for only a select few? Kreeft points out that saints are not "far-out freaks, weirdos, or exceptions. They are the rule, the plumb line, the standard operating model for human beings. If we are *not* saints, we are the exceptions to the rule...." Then he goes on to give us a magnificent description of those who are successful in this quest for holiness.

> What is a saint? A saint is first of all one who knows he is a sinner. A saint knows all the news, both the bad news of sin and the good news of salvation. A saint is a true scientist, a true philosopher: a saint knows the Truth. A saint is a seer, one who sees what is there. A saint is a realist.

A saint is also an idealist. A saint embraces heroic suffering out of heroic love. A saint also embraces heroic joy.[1]

Saints are people who have allowed God to restore his own image within them. They are repentant sinners, who with true realism give themselves completely to the love of God in Christ. Saints are willing to give up everything, even life itself, for the love of Christ. A saint is willing to embrace heroic suffering so as to experience heroic joy. As St. Paul says, "Not that I complain of want; for I have learned, in whatever state I am, to be content. I know how to be abased, and I know how to abound; in any and all circumstances I have learned the secret of facing plenty and hunger, abundance and want. I can do all things in him who strengthens me" (Phil 4:11-13).

Saints are quintessentially stubborn, people so closed-minded and determined that they will die before compromising the truth of God. They come in all shapes and sizes. Some may be conservative, old-fashioned, and tough; others may be liberal, urbane, and kindly. But when it comes to holiness and obedience to God, saints are narrow-minded and uncompromising.

Consider St. Thomas More, a sophisticated and highly educated man. The son of an attorney, he himself became known as the most kind, just, skilled, and popular judge in London. More could deal with strange things that didn't seem to fit, a lot of confusion, and issues that went backwards, forwards, and sideways. He could find a way to deal with people that others didn't know what to do with. Although he had to be aware that the king was a disturbed man, he continued to serve him and the state.

Then the king overstepped a line drawn by More. When the pope denied King Henry VIII an annulment of his marriage to Catherine of Aragon, Henry became so infuriated that he maneuvered a separation from Rome. He then declared that he was the supreme head of the Church of England.

Thomas More was shocked that King Henry would claim such a position. Also, as the Lord Chancellor, he refused to acknowledge the validity of the king's divorce, and resigned his post. In

1534, the Act of Supremacy was passed, requiring an oath by all the king's subjects acknowledging that the royal union with Anne Boleyn was valid and their offspring legitimate heirs to the throne. A refusal to take the oath was considered high treason.

Many Catholics took the oath with the private reservation, "so far as it be not contrary to the law of God." But when it came to the truths of salvation, Thomas More became immovable. He was willing to die rather than compromise. On the doctrine of the church and apostolic succession, he was intransigent. More was eventually found guilty of high treason and beheaded in 1535. His final words were, "I call you to witness, brothers, that I die in and for the faith of the Catholic Church; the king's loyal servant, but God's first."

A BEAUTIFUL COUNTRY ESTATE?

It is an error to think that we can *arrive* at perfect holiness. The fact is that we arrive at very little in this life—besides the cemetery. Almost anything else that we achieve is a moving target. Whatever possessions we accumulate are in the process of being lost fairly soon.

The minute we purchase any longed-for possession like a new house or car, it begins to depreciate, rust, or rot. Even if we take excellent care of a car, it inevitably receives that first scratch. Jesus warns us not to lay up treasures on earth, "but lay up for yourselves treasures in heaven, where neither moth nor rust consumes and where thieves do not break in and steal. For where your treasure is, there will your heart be also" (Mt 6:20-21).

People like to think of holiness as some beautiful country estate someplace over the hills where they will arrive some day... if they stay around long enough. Devout young people in their twenties and thirties mistakenly believe they will soon arrive at this blessed estate. Those in their forties and fifties and sixties are starting to wonder. Holiness is beginning to recede way off in the distance. Anyone in their seventies or eighties knows the awful truth: *one never arrives at the state of holiness.* As a matter of fact, holiness becomes even more elusive as we make progress.

I could offer many common examples to prove this point. Perfectly coiffeured hair is not something you arrive at forevermore. If you clean your house so that it's spotless, will it still be clean two or three weeks later? No, of course not. In even another few days, the dirt and dust will have started to accumulate again. Weeding the garden, clearing the driveway, or repairing the car or the house is a constant, ongoing process.

Holiness is like that. We never arrive at the state of perfect repair and purity. It is always out there ahead of us. There is always more that needs to be done. If you just completed a marvelous, thirty-day retreat, and then made the best confession of your entire lifetime, complete with a heavy penance... I've got news for you. The next day, you would be getting ready for your next confession. So would I.

The day I made my final vows was a miserable one for me. I really wasn't enthused about the prospect, but knew I had to do it because the Lord had called me to this vocation. St. Thomas Aquinas teaches that a person making final vows receives *baptismal innocence*—meaning the soul is all polished like a golden chalice. Doesn't that sound nice? Well, let me assure you, it wasn't for me.

When I arrived at the ceremony, I consoled myself with, "Well, at least I'm going to get baptismal innocence." Fr. Lambert preached an upbeat sermon on the three vows being the "three nails in the cross." I thought disconsolately that our Lord hung on the cross for only three hours, while I had about fifty years to go!

Before the end of the liturgy, I found myself upset about something that had gone wrong. I could feel a surge of anger welling up inside. As I got back to the sacristy, I sighed, "Well, so much for baptismal innocence!" I didn't even make it off the altar before the chalice of my soul had been tarnished by an ugly smudge down the side. But I had the peace of knowing I had stayed only because I believed God was able to do with me what he said he would do.

ENEMIES WITHOUT AND WITHIN

Holiness is a long pilgrimage—a very long one. To understand that trip best is to understand that the life of a Christian is a battle, a spiritual combat. Contemporary theology often leads us to believe that everything has to be "peachy." Haven't you heard those sermons about "positive thinking" and "creation spirituality"? The preacher promises everything will be wonderful. As soon as you get rid of your inhibitions, repressions, and neurotic defense mechanisms, you'll absolutely glow in the dark!

If that's the message you're seeking, you won't hear it from me. What I'm going to tell you about is a perilous spiritual warfare that goes on in the soul with countless enemies from the world, the flesh, and the devil.

To be "of this world" involves any use of creation apart from its relationship to God as our final destiny. To be "of this world" is to live apart from God. The flesh, on the other hand, refers to our physical appetites and biological desires. The commandments of God guide us in controlling the cravings of our flesh.

Some contemporary Christians say that they are at peace with the world, that they don't think Christians should be unworldly. People who don't see the necessity of spiritual combat have themselves usually been drawn deep into worldliness. The saint strives to be totally faithful to Christ and totally dependent on him. Christ must come first.

What of the devil or Satan? He is a malign, independent, invisible being who is fended off by our intelligent use of spiritual means. Both Scripture and Catholic Tradition affirm Satan's existence and that of other fallen spirits, or fallen angels, who tempt us and disrupt our lives. These other fallen angels have submitted themselves to the sovereignty of Satan. Their activities are most often subtle, but in extreme instances, like the cruelties imposed by the Nazis and Bolsheviks, their influence is palpable. Heights of evil, such as those manifested during the Holocaust, can be accounted for only by the realization that powers beyond those of human nature, were at work.

Our struggle against the devil, is more obvious than the battle against worldliness. We are warned to be sober and watchful because our adversary, the devil, is prowling around like a roaring lion, seeking someone to devour. "Resist him, firm in your faith, knowing that the same experience of suffering is required of your brotherhood throughout the world. And after you have suffered a little while, the God of all grace, who has called you to his eternal glory in Christ, will himself restore, establish, and strengthen you" (1 Pt 5:9-10).

Though we are all in a constant spiritual battle against worldliness and the devil, it seems to me that the biggest and most persistent enemy is always *self*, that dangerous Trojan horse within the gates. Have you ever tried the "geographic cure" for some chronic problem like alcoholism or depression—that is, changing jobs or moving to another city? The problem is, you have to take yourself along with you. You can never escape yourself; you can only change yourself.

I recall Frank Sheed's eightieth birthday. Someone asked if he would like to be twenty-one again. Sheed replied, "I wouldn't even like to be seventy-nine again!" This reflected his healthy perspective on life and eternity. Why go back? Life is a battle, sometimes hand-to-hand combat. Frank was never one to try to escape from himself. He cheerfully fought on and died a very saintly man. Frank understood God's work of salvation.

We may thank God for whatever pain and suffering already lies behind us. St. Paul sums up the quest for holiness in these words: "Not that I have already obtained this or am already perfect; but I press on to make it my own, because Christ Jesus has made me his own. Brethren, I do not consider that I have made it my own; but one thing I do, forgetting what lies behind and straining forward to what lies ahead, I press on toward the goal for the prize of the upward call of God in Christ Jesus" (Phil 3:12-14).

WHOM DO WE PUT FIRST IN OUR LIVES?

Our part in this spiritual battle is to put God first in our lives. Much easier said than done, of course. All of us are tempted to put ourselves first. Many people have someone in their lives whom they love so dearly that they put that person before themselves. You who are wives, husbands, mothers, and fathers certainly know what I mean. Some people are so fed up with themselves and others that they might feel closer to God than anyone else... but he still seems very far away.

You hurt people or cheat people by putting them before God. You may destroy them or come close to doing so. Parents who put their children before God are doing them no favor. Spouses who put their mates before God inevitably live unsatisfying lives. Nothing and no one can come before God.

Sometimes we experience genuine conflict when we truly love and want the very best for someone. St. Thomas More faced such a struggle because of his wife. Should he hold firm to the truth and leave her a widow? His wife, who certainly didn't want her husband to die a martyr, made various intelligent suggestions as to how he could avoid such a fate. But More did what he had to do to stand up for the truth, regardless of the consequences. This faithful husband left his wife and children in the hands of God, the very best place for anyone to be.

Another saint of that time was old Bishop John Fisher. He felt the people needed the example of a spiritual leader who didn't leave King Henry VIII any way out. So he told Henry in so many words, to go jump in the lake. "I refuse. I will not sign the oath. It is heresy, utter nonsense. If you want to behead me, go sharpen the axe."

St. Thomas More, being a good husband and father, didn't rush out and volunteer to become a martyr. But when push came to shove, when he saw no other way, he was intractable.

Can you imagine what More's life and that of his family would have been like if he had wavered at the last minute—whether out of fear of death or out of concern for his family? How miserable to have the ignominy of being honored by Henry VIII! The men who carried out the king's orders and put More to death, Cromwell and Cramner, were both executed within a few years.

Sometimes when we think we are putting a person or God

first, it just isn't so. That's one of the tricks of human nature. The truth is that we are often putting ourselves first through self-indulgence in our relationship with the other person.

Many people complain to me about being lonely. As a psychologist, I know there are worse problems than loneliness. One of them is being married to the wrong person. I know many people who would much prefer to end a particular relationship and be lonely for a while. There are very good mothers who would appreciate more time alone without young children constantly under foot.

Loneliness, however, is one of those painful realities of life that drives people into the arms of God. Sooner or later, loneliness comes to almost everyone. The most loving couple who have been blessed with a Christian marriage must eventually say goodbye. Their sorrow will be as great as their mutual fulfillment has been.

We all ultimately must put God first. Everybody—including people like Nicholas Lenin, Joseph Stalin, Adolph Hitler, Joseph Goebbels, and Saddam Hussein. When these particular men are summoned before the judgment seat of God, will God be first? Certainly! And if they are found guilty in the eyes of God, then their own personal judgment will be that they knew they were doing it and yet continued to put themselves first anyway.

Such is our own struggle. Will we put God first, where he rightfully belongs? Or will we yield to the world, the devil, and the flesh, and try to put ourselves first? If we make the wrong choice, the consequences will always be negative. Sooner or later, for better or for worse, we will reap what we sow. God holds us responsible for our thoughts and actions.

A JEWISH MOTHER

You cannot put anything before the love of God. We must put God first even when it is painful to do so. An unparalleled example is the Virgin Mary, who had to balance her human love for her Son with the demands of his mysterious mission and her own call to sanctity.

We know from Scripture and Tradition that Jesus had no physical father. His human nature came wholly from Mary. Mary and Jesus must have been startlingly similar in appearance. They shared many things that nobody else could share, that even Joseph couldn't comprehend. On the other hand, the Son had experiences that were totally beyond his mother.

We also know that this extraordinary relationship had room for disagreements. Two of them are recorded: one at the finding of the child Jesus in the temple, and the other at the marriage feast of Cana. Somehow or another, in the midst of all the mystery of Jesus' parentage, we can see a vestige of the Jewish mother with her boy—"my Son, the Messiah."

Nonetheless, we clearly see that on both sides, God's will came first. We see that choice carried to the extreme as Jesus hung on the cross. Earlier in his ministry, Jesus had revealed his commitment to God's preeminence when someone ran up to tell him that his mother and brothers were waiting outside for him. Jesus answered, "Who is my mother, and who are my brethren?... For whoever does the will of my Father in heaven is my brother, and sister, and mother" (Mt 12:48-50).

At Calvary, this commitment is played out in its most awful dimensions. Jesus' mother is present, but speaks not a word. The farewell between mother and Son is given in some mysterious form which we cannot see or hear. Right next to the Holy Sepulcher in Jerusalem stands the Chapel of the Apparition of the Risen Christ to the Blessed Virgin. We Franciscans cannot believe for one moment that Christ did not appear first to his mother—though it is not recorded in Scripture.

Ponder the drama of holiness at the cross. Here are the only two people untouched by original sin, and one of them with two natures—divine and human. Even there, we see the struggle to put God first.

Mary loved Christ in two ways. As the mother of his human nature and physical body, she loved him as her own Son. She loved Jesus as God, as the Messiah and Savior of the world. Mary watched helplessly as Jesus carried his cross down the Via Dolorosa. Her mother's heart must have broken as the nails were pounded into his flesh and she endured the torment of being unable to comfort him. She watched as callous soldiers threw dice for the seamless garment which she herself had probably woven. How utterly alone and wretched she must have felt!

In such depths of pain, Mary remained faithful to her primary dedication to God. She did not cling to Jesus or beg for mercy. She stood and watched with John, rather than run away like the other disciples. Mary accepted John as her son as Jesus indicated from the cross. She agreed to go on living and serving the budding community of disciples.

Of course, our Blessed Mother was pierced to the heart by the suffering which obedience entailed. No one ever said that sanctity was going to be easy. But as the French writer Léon Bloy wrote, "Life holds only one tragedy, ultimately not to have been a saint." Mary clung to the one thing that was necessary: loving God with all of her heart, soul, and mind.

EVEN THE SAINTS STRUGGLE

Don't grow discouraged by your own struggles. All the saints had their troubles. Mother Seton saw most of her children die of the same tuberculosis that caused her own premature death. Bernadette and Thérèse of Lisieux both died painful deaths early in life.

Don't think that anyone arrives at such a level of holiness in this life that they rise above sin or temptation. The greatest of saints will tell you that they are poor sinners. I do think that many more people arrive at sanctification than most of us assume. I have even met people outside of Christianity who, through the great mercy of God and his providence, seemed to be in touch with the grace of Christ... *whom they did not even know*. Christ is, after all is said and done, the Savior and Lord of all.

St. Paul was well aware that his followers and converts wanted to be holy and put God first. He also knew that they would grow discouraged. Paul's poignant prayer on behalf of the Colossians, gives a vivid description of the struggle for holiness:

> And so, from the day we heard of it, we have not ceased to pray for you, asking that you may be filled with the knowledge of his will in all spiritual wisdom and understanding, to lead a life worthy of the Lord, fully pleasing to him, bearing fruit in every good work and increasing in the knowledge of God. May you be strengthened with all power, according to his glorious might, for all endurance and patience with joy, giving thanks to the Father, who has qualified us to share in the inheritance of the saints in light. He has delivered us from the dominion of darkness and transferred us to the kingdom of his beloved Son, in whom we have redemption, the forgiveness of sins. **Col 1:9-14**

I don't know about you, but I get very discouraged when I think about sanctity. Having known people who have consistently and heroically pursued the will of God. I feel like I am barely shilly-shallying along the way.

Perhaps you're thinking, "Ah, but you're a priest. You are closer to spiritual things; you even live with the Blessed Sacrament. You have many more opportunities for sanctity than I do." Believe me, I am very well aware of that fact, and it makes me feel all the more humbled and responsible. But I'll be very honest with you: I'm just like everyone else. My natural human tendency is to put myself first.

Even the greatest of saints had his or her own human weakness—or else they wouldn't have been human beings. Sin more often enters the picture in our own disproportionate reaction to another's traits or pecularities. You know that the apostles got put off by their Master more than once.

I have known a few people who have a very good chance of being canonized—well enough to know their ups and downs and ins and outs. There were little things, which most people wouldn't see as faults at all. Take my dear friend, Cardinal Cooke, for example. He was a saintly, holy man...but a fuss-budget when it came to cleanliness. You could catch him once in a while blowing the dust off the furniture. I, of course, am an utter slob, so his fastidiousness bothered me.

Cardinal Cooke met me in the elevator one day when I was wearing a black suit and a Roman collar. He said, "Benedict, what have you got on?" I answered, "Well, I'm sorry to tell you, this is my black suit." He said, "You look awful." And I've hardly ever worn a black suit since. Instead, I dress in my Franciscan habit. Until that time we were told that friars couldn't wear their habits in public. I have it on the authority of the archbishop of New York that I look better in one. (Of course, that doesn't say much for the suit.)

When you get to know someone well, it's impossible not to see the little toad of self-indulgence or self-love sticking its head out of his or her personality from time to time. Don't wait to find a person who has no foibles. You'll never find anyone who goes through life always happy, smiling, and filled with joy, peace, and charity. There are no such people in real life, only in phony books or rosy TV sitcoms.

Time was, most Catholics thought that to be canonized a saint, a person had to be known to have no faults. That's ridiculous! To be canonized a saint, it has to be proven that a person practiced *heroic virtue*. The very definition of *heroic* implies that it was a terrible struggle... and that once in a while the person probably didn't make it!

I remember being told a story about a great Capuchin, Fr. Stephen Ecker, and his scolding of a friar, a very good man who was an absolute extrovert with the worst social judgment imaginable. If there was a wrong way to say something, Fr. Innocent would say it. On the feast of Corpus Christi, he was invited to dinner with Cardinal Farley. Someone foolishly sat him next to the cardinal.

During dinner, Fr. Innocent said, "Your Grace, have you heard that because of the Humane Society, a policeman cannot shoot a dog with a broken leg?" Incredulous, Cardinal Farley innocently repeated to everyone else, "Reverend Fathers, have you heard about that foolish Humane Society, that because of them a policeman cannot shoot a dog with a broken leg?"

Then Fr. Innocent blurted out, "He has to shoot him with a gun! Ha! Ha!" Cardinal Farley was not amused. From that day to the day of his death fifty-seven years later, Fr. Innocent would not walk past St. Patrick's Cathedral. He always walked around the block.

One day—at the end of his patience I would imagine—Fr. Stephen told Innocent to behave. Fifty years after this rebuke, Fr. Innocent was called to testify in the cause of Fr. Stephen's beatification. When he returned from testifying, Fr. Innocent told us, "I can't tell you nothing. I had to take an oath so I can't tell you a thing. But I'll say this: it ain't going to go well." I assure you, his testimony did nothing to support the cause of Fr. Stephen.

We must reject the phony image of holiness. A saint is just a sinner who is more repentant than most of us. If there is any place for perfection in our lives, it is perfect contrition for our sins. *Perfect contrition* is grief of the soul because we have offended God who is infinitely good, coupled with a firm resolve to cease offending him. *Imperfect contrition* is sorrow for our sins because we know we have been caught and fear the punishment due to them. A little boy caught with his hand in the cookie jar is a good example. Most of us are a mixture of holiness and selfishness, and hopefully we grow in grace and love of God as we mature in our spiritual lives. Some of us unfortunately never grow enough to take responsibility for our failings.

The journey to holiness begins anew every day when we begin to see some fault of our own, some egotism, some narcissism, some self-pity, something we haven't yet given up. Whether it looks great or small to others, it can look like a seven-storey mountain to us. We will despair of ever getting past such a huge barrier... until slowly the grace of God shows us the only clear path over it. And then we begin the arduous climb—picking up one foot and putting it in front of the other, one labored step at a time.

The road to holiness doesn't sound easy, does it? It's not.

Only by the grace of God can we successfully complete the journey.

REACHING THE END OF OUR ROPE

Healing the original wound is no easy task. You might ask, "How do we go about this process of sanctification? What are the rules of the journey?" I would like to offer the advice of one of my favorite people who is now being considered for beatification: Cardinal John Henry Newman.

An energetic, apostolic minister of the Anglican Church, Newman had a very difficult life. In the parish of Littlemore where he was a priest, I met an old woman whose family had known him. She told me that when he died forty-five years after he had left Littlemore to become a Catholic, the Sunday service at the Anglican parish was filled with people in tears because of Cardinal Newman's death. How had he so long-endeared himself to those people?

Newman gives us a hint. He wrote the advice below when he was living in Ireland and finding disaster wherever he turned. He went there to establish the Catholic University of Ireland and never succeeded. As he said, "Every door was closed to me." Newman was very sensitive. Much of his life as a Catholic he was criticized, just as he had been as an Anglican. It wasn't until he was very old that he was made a cardinal by Pope Leo XIII. On that occasion, Newman said, "The clouds have lifted."

Newman called his instructions "the short road to perfection."

It is the saying of holy men that, if we wish to be perfect, we have nothing more to do than perform the ordinary duties of the day well. A short road to perfection—short, not because easy, but because pertinent and intelligible. There are no easy ways to perfection, but there are sure ones.

I think this is an instruction which may be of great practical use to persons like ourselves. It is easy to have vague ideas of what perfection is, which serve well enough to talk about, when we do not intend to aim at it; but as soon as a person really desires and sets about seeking it himself, he is dissatisfied with anything but what is tangible and clear, and constitutes some sort of direction toward the practice of it.

We must bear in mind what is meant by perfection. It does not mean any extraordinary service, anything out of the way, or especially heroic—not all have the opportunity of heroic acts, of sufferings—but it means what the word perfection ordinarily means. By perfect we mean that which has no flaw in it, that which is complete, that which is consistent, that which is sound—we mean the opposite to imperfect. As we all know well what *im*perfection in religious service means, we know by the contrast what is meant by perfection.

He, then, is perfect who does the work of the day perfectly, and we need not go beyond this to seek for perfection. You need not go out of the *round* of the day.

I insist on this because it will simplify our views, and fix our exertions on a definite aim. If you ask me what you are to do in order to be perfect, I say, first—Do not lie in bed beyond the due time of rising; give your first thoughts to God; make a good visit to the Blessed Sacrament; say the Angelus; eat and drink to God's glory; say the Rosary well; be recollected; keep out bad thoughts; make your evening meditation well; examine yourself daily; go to bed in good time, and you are already perfect.[2]

Cardinal Newman also says that perfection is based on the three great theological virtues of faith, hope, and charity. Perfectly manifesting them is never easy—living within the confines of our fallen human nature, surrounded by our own weaknesses in a troubled world.

We all experience slips and falls. We all must rely on the grace of God to rise up and press on. The Holy Spirit helps us when we have reached the end of our rope. The Holy Spirit enlightens our darkness and strengthens us.

Our part is to cry out to God to fill us with the knowledge of his will, with all the wisdom and understanding that his Spirit gives. Only then will we be able to live as the Lord wants and do what is pleasing to him.

Christians need to read and practice what is taught in Scripture, especially in the Gospels. Christians need prayerfully to serve others. God has been particularly gracious to the Catholic Church. We have already discussed the gift of apostolic succession, the sacraments, and the loving support of brothers and sisters. The church offers us some specific means to personal sanctity:

1. The Holy Eucharist, especially at daily Mass.
2. Daily prayer, especially in the presence of Christ before the Blessed Sacrament.
3. Frequent reception of the Sacrament of Reconciliation.
4. Daily examination of conscience.
5. Making friends with Our Lady and the saints who have gone before us.

ALWAYS BECOMING

Psychology is often not very helpful in matters concerning the spiritual life. But I do find it helpful in explaining this truth: in this life we are never finally something; we are always *becoming*. We are never stuck; we are always growing. It just may not seem that way sometimes, since human growth can be as imperceptible as that of the trees and grass and flowers. We may be becoming a lot of things—good, bad, mediocre, stuck, or unstuck—but we are always becoming.

One of my favorite groups is Alcoholics Anonymous, a splendid organization with a solid spiritual foundation. You will never hear anybody get up at an AA meeting and say, "My name is Charlie. I used to be an alcoholic, but now I'm sober. I'm an ex-alcoholic." When they introduce themselves, they describe themselves as simply an "alcoholic" or a "recovering alcoholic."

You might ask, "Well, when are you going to completely

recover?" When we're dead, they will tell you. *Recovering* is a word like *becoming*. It captures the sense of *process*. An AA member could honestly say, "I'm *becoming* a sober person." Sobriety means learning how to think, act, and talk, without the influence of alcohol.

So it is with holiness. "Hello, my name is Benedict. I'm a *recovering* sinner. I'm *becoming* a saint." When anybody tells you that they *are* a saint... RUN, do not walk, to the nearest exit. People like that are all over the place, especially in states like California and New York. Sometimes they get locked up with the crazy people. Sometimes they run for elected office.

Isn't it astounding that our ordinary, everyday, disappointing, oftentimes dull, happenstance lives—even while burdened down with sorrow and pain—are filled by the grace of our Lord Jesus Christ? That he can take our cracked earthen pots and make us holy?

When I was trying to prepare one young man with AIDS for death, I told him the story of the good thief (see Lk 23:32-39). Having been convicted of robbery, he was hanging on a cross on one side of our Lord. The criminal on the other side blasted Jesus for not saving himself and them.

The robber knew death was fast approaching. He didn't have much time to repent, to repair the wrongdoing which had put him on the cross. Gathering all his strength, the good thief said to his fellow criminal, "You and I are here because of what we have done, but this man is innocent. Remember me, Lord, when you come into your kingdom."

Faith, hope, and love were captured in those few words. Jesus replied to the first canonized saint of the church, "Today you will be with me in paradise." As long as we have one more breath to draw, there is hope for our salvation.

Becoming holy is God's work in us. It has been said that our goal is not to be good, but to be God's. I think that sums up the struggle. Holiness is God's work in us which we grasp through faith, hope, and charity. Sanctification for the Christian is the work of Christ in the soul.

But it is always a becoming, a process, a journey. Holiness is always ahead, somewhere around the next bend... until we round the final corner and come face to face with the Lord in heaven. We are becoming saints.

◆ ◆ ◆

O Lord Jesus Christ, you alone know the holiness of God and the weakness of humanity. You alone have dwelt in the heavens and on the earth. Though without sin, you have borne our infirmities and tasted the bitter effects of our evil deeds. You call us to be holy so that we may pass on to that holy life which is without any change or sorrow, to that place of endless day where there is no mourning or crying anymore. You have gone before us and sent the Advocate to stand beside us in our trials.

O Divine Master, call us ever more powerfully to follow you on the way of holiness. Call us to sanctification by your life and death, by your Word and sacraments. Save those who are dear to us. Save those who have strayed away. Call to those who are perishing because you have died for us all. And make us by your grace witnesses to your salvation and holiness in this world in which we struggle on, guided by the light shining from your cross. Amen.

SEVEN

The Door to Eternity

When the perishable puts on the imperishable, and the mortal puts on immortality, then shall come to pass the saying that is written:

> *"Death is swallowed up in victory."*
> *"O death, where is thy victory?*
> *O death, where is thy sting?"* 1 Cor 15:54-55

I RECENTLY VISITED A YOUNG Puerto Rican who was dying of AIDS. I had known him and his family since he was a little child, and had even celebrated the fiftieth anniversary of his grandparents in Harlem. This twenty-nine-year-old man contracted AIDS from a hypodermic needle. Now his wife is a widow and his young child is fatherless.

I had not seen Willy over the years, despite my frequent contact with his parents and family. He had gone into the streets and led a wild life. When I heard he had tested HIV positive, I went to see him and made it clear that he had to "clean up his act." Willy received the sacraments after making a heartfelt examination of conscience, and faithfully continued to follow God until his death more than a year later.

Some months after Willy's return to the faith, I was talking to him about the spiritual journey that lay ahead. Willy was not exactly prepared, but since it would soon be time for him to go home to God, I was trying to help him make up for lost time. He had learned the hard way that life is spiritual warfare that affects everyone and must be fought individually and corporately. I wanted to assure him that death need not be frightening, though he was both scared and angry.

"Willy," I said, "it will be hard for you to believe this, but I might die before you because I have heart trouble. If I knew that I was going to die before you, I wouldn't be so sad, because I know what lies ahead. Purgatory, as the saints tell us, is a vast improvement over this situation, especially if you live in New York City. It'll definitely be like moving to the Upper East Side, like going from Fort Apache to the Silk Stocking District." I hope he believed me. I went on to tell Willy what I could about heaven—"what eye has not seen, nor ear heard."

When I visited him a few weeks later, he looked like death was upon him. "Willy, are you frightened?" This was the wrong question to ask a tough city kid.

That young man answered, "I'm not frightened at all! Me? Not me! You told me Jesus is waiting for me. So why should I be frightened?" Willy was prepared for death. He died a few weeks later, surrounded by his family, holding the hand of a Redemptorist priest, and singing hymns. The Lord had given him the grace to be ready.

WHAT COMES NEXT?

The mystery and certainty of death pose gigantic questions. What comes next? Where are we going? What are we ultimately going to be? We have been reflecting on the glorious truths of salvation primarily in terms of this earthly life. Yet the original wound will never be completely healed as long as the earth groans in travail. We can never achieve heaven on earth, no matter how hard we try.

Though nothing in life is more certain, death is a topic most people avoid approaching head-on. Very sick people are quickly trundled off to the hospital to "pass away," and often, not for lack of caring. "Putting the deceased to rest" is filled with denial. Remarks like, "Doesn't he look good? They did such a wonderful job with his make-up!"—can sound silly at a wake.

Funerals are meant to be awesome, solemn events, full of sorrow, especially for loved ones and close friends. If you come to mine, don't sing "alleluia." Please, at least pretend you're sorry. I don't want any bubbles or balloons or anything like them at my funeral. No alleluias. I'll wait for the resurrection.

How do you see death? How do you foresee your destiny?

Children are usually afraid of death. It seems like a terribly big thing, full of mystery. I remember my first funeral. When an Orthodox Jewish lady in our neighborhood died, I went to "sit shiva" for her with my grandmother. The mirrors and pictures were covered with newspaper. The little benches were filled with shoeless mourners wailing traditional Jewish lamentations.

I also remember how awesome my great grandmother's funeral seemed. Bigger than life. I was only ten and wanted her to speak to me, even though I knew she couldn't. I just couldn't believe that I wouldn't see her again until I was old and died myself.

When I became an altar boy, death started to take on a different perspective. We buried the great and the small. We learned a lot about life carrying candles and crucifixes out to the cemetery. The motherhouse of Dominican sisters in our town was always sending elderly sisters shuffling off to God. Twice a month I'd be up there with bell, book, and candle to carry out dear old Sister Imelda or Sister Andrea.

I grew accustomed to the process, but since I didn't know any of the sisters in the infirmary, I never stopped to think of any of the people we buried as having actually been alive. And by the time I got there, the dear sisters were already stone cold. Then one day when I was on my way to do a chore in the motherhouse, I saw a car pull up. The driver took out a box and a small, elderly nun got out. "Sister, can I help you?" I asked. She said yes and told me she had been stationed in Rutherford.

"You're going to be here now?"

"That's right."

"Where will you go from here?" She looked me straight in the eye and replied with a thick German accent, "Grand Central Station."

I carried the cardboard box upstairs, which must have contained all her belongings. Then it dawned on me: this nun was talking about her own death. She wasn't going to move off this floor until I got her as an altar boy! As it turned out, this sister didn't die until after I went on to high school, so I didn't actually assist at her funeral. But connecting the reality of death with a warm body made death seem still more awesome.

With the fall of the human race, death entered the world, and with it, darkness, fear, and pain. People can die young, cut down by disease, accident, or violence. Without a clear sense of our destiny, leaving this world remains a curse, a deep sorrow—especially when a person dies prematurely.

What does happen after life, after death? Certainly not oblivion. Anthropology marks the beginning of human beings as we know them by the existence of grave sites filled with tools and utensils commonly employed during life. A large amount of pottery suggests that food and drink were also left in the tombs, perhaps in preparation for a journey. Even though these people may have lived very differently than any of us can imagine, they evidently anticipated passing on to another existence.

The oldest buildings on the face of the earth, the pyramids, offer graphic evidence of the human hope for life after death. The ancient Egyptians had a vested interest in constructing the pyramids and stocking them with food and drink, gold coins and jewelry, and weapons. They believed that if the pharaoh survived death, then the common people would make the passage as well. The elaborate paintings on the walls of the pyramids make this clear.

That ancient intuition of the ruler as the head of the people is analogous to the mystical body of Christ. We are saved not only *because* of Christ, we are saved *in and through* him. Those who die in the state of grace are actually part of his mystical body. Ancient people thought of their rulers in somewhat the same way.

AFTERLIFE EXPERIENCES

Recently psychologists have been studying so-called "after-life" experiences. Some people believe in life after death because of stories told by those who have suffered clinical death and come back to tell about it. Perhaps you even know someone who has had such an experience. The accounts often describe walking through a tunnel to a light or walking across a bridge in the mist, then frequently meeting a close friend or relative who has been deceased for a while.

One of my friends was the most unpoetic, unimaginative priest I have ever met—as plain as a mud fence. He suffered a heart attack in the rectory, a second one in the ambulance, and a third one in the emergency room. The hospital "coded" him as dead. But God decided to fool them all. Fr. Tony slowly came back to life.

When I dropped in to visit him several days later, he said, "You know, Benedict, it's a funny thing. I didn't even know I had a heart attack. I was just unconscious. Then I was walking out on this bridge covered with fog and I saw my friend, Fr. Vincent, coming toward me through the fog. I said, 'Hey, Vinny, you're supposed to be dead. What are you doing here?' And he walked up to me and he smiled. Then he started to back away. That's all I remember."

That was Fr. Tony's life-after-death experience. This most unimaginative person had never heard of such a phenomenon. I myself do not believe in life after death because of such stories, but they are interesting. Why do I believe in life after death? Because Christ has revealed it.

DEATH IS NOT THE END

Multitudes now and in ages past have hoped for and believed in life after death. Perhaps they see the injustice and the misery which is the lot of so many on this earth. Even non-Christians often expect an inevitable balancing of the accounts of life by the good and provident force which brought the world into existence.

Others believe in life after death because of the intrinsic value of the human being—not in the abstract sense, but out of a very concrete love for someone. They naturally desire to be rejoined with those whom they love, in another world. When you look at the hollow shell of a dead body, you somehow intuitively know that the spirit of the person has moved on. Where to?

I have a very good friend who is a physician. He and his wife were atheists, but fine, concerned, decent, hardworking human beings. She was dying of a debilitating disease. My friend said to me, "I wish she could live four hundred years."

I said, "No, you don't. You wish she could live forever."

"Yes," he truthfully answered, "I wish she could live forever."

That aspiration to live forever reaches throughout the human race. Go wherever you will and find any religion, and you will find people hoping that this life is not all that there is. Even though they may have a different concept than Christianity about everlasting life, they hope that death is not the end.

Does wishing make it so? No, but I believe such a common aspiration must be indicative of some profound, intrinsic value of the human soul. Many spiritual people throughout the world religions—mystics, seers, prophets, scholars—have claimed to have been in touch with the world beyond the grave. Almost every major world religion teaches that the individual survives death. Even in nontheistic belief systems, popular opinion proclaims an afterlife.

We also see a common belief in life after death in terms of divine judgment. Those who do evil are warned in every world religion that their destiny after death will be punishment. Our

Lord Jesus Christ warns people repeatedly to be ready, to watch, to be prepared. Death will come like a thief in the night. All persons will be rewarded according to their own deeds. (See especially the parables in Matthew 24 and 25.)

The Christian belief in life after death is founded first and foremost on the bodily resurrection of Jesus, and his promise that his disciples would join him in his Father's house. Jesus thus became the door to eternal life. He prepares a way for us. He often taught about this truth, not only to warn people to prepare for death but also to enable them to go through the doors of death into the kingdom of God.

Jesus Christ came into the world to transform death by his resurrection. The pattern of human life had been predictable, with birth leading to growth, then decline, followed by death. Then a human being came back to life who would never die again. A being totally different, a singularity, without scientific explanation. Indeed, something that religion can scarcely deal with: the prospect of eternal life.

I suppose Jesus Christ could have risen from the dead another way. He could have chosen to be merely an apparition, with his body staying in the tomb while his spirit reappeared, just as the saints and Old Testament prophets have appeared. If it had happened that way, we would have been satisfied. We still would have been assured of life after death.

But that's not what happened. What took place flew against all the laws of nature. A particle of this material world that had once been a living man, died a gruesome death. The stone cold body of Jesus spent three days in the tomb. That body did not decay, but incredibly came back to life. The Christ who appeared to the apostles and the disciples was not an apparition or a ghost. He ate a fish. Thomas stuck his hand into our Lord's wounds. As Peter Kreeft says:

Christianity is the religion of the conquest of death. Christ came to change death from an enemy to a friend, from a hole to a door, from a juggernaut to the golden chariot sent by the King to fetch his beloved Cinderella-bride to his castle to live with him forever. The Christian can stick his tongue out at death and give it a Bronx cheer, like St. Paul: "Oh death, where is thy sting? Oh grave, where is thy victory?" "The sting of death is sin," and death is now a stingless bee, for its stinger has lodged in the body of Christ on the Cross.[1]

The bodily resurrection of Christ is utterly mysterious, beyond any expectation of the human mind. Your job and mine as baptized Christians is to declare to others our belief in this glorious reality.

Jesus foretold his death and resurrection several times, accounts which were mostly unintelligible to his disciples except in retrospect. After his resurrection, our Lord appeared bodily on several occasions until he ascended into heaven. The testimony of the church began less than twenty years after the death of Jesus.

The oldest Christian document as far as we know is the First Epistle to the Thessalonians, in which St. Paul clearly and authoritatively speaks about eternal life: "For since we believe that Jesus died and rose again, even so, through Jesus, God will bring with him those who have fallen asleep.... And the dead in Christ will rise first; then we who are alive, who are left, shall be caught up together with them in the clouds to meet the Lord in the air; and so we shall always be with the Lord. Therefore comfort one another with these words" (1 Thes 4:14-18).

THE ETERNAL COCKTAIL PARTY

Do we comfort each other with the words of truth, or do we offer only empty platitudes? I was once invited to speak at a prestigious medical school on the topic of "grief and loss." I asked, "Well, what grief are you talking about and what loss are you considering?" I already knew what they meant; I just couldn't help needling them a bit.

The organizers of the conference were a bit flustered by my question. After hemming and hawing, they stammered, "Well, when someone dies... expires." In a hospital, nobody dies; they just expire. I said, "So let's talk about it." I rolled up my sleeves to join this very distinguished group, which included a minister, rabbi, psychiatrist, and psychologist, as well as medical professionals.

While looking depressed at the prospect, these folks proceeded to philosophize about the acceptance of death. One of their points was that all the troubles of life prepare us for death. They are all "little deaths" in a sense.

That's certainly true. By the time you reach my age, the news of your impending demise could be met with a fair amount of enthusiasm. I wouldn't be at all troubled to check out. As I mentioned in the last chapter, I'm actually looking forward to moving from the Bronx to the post-mortem Upper East Side. Purgatory will definitely rank as a step up in my life.

Anyway, what I found most interesting was the fact that no one wanted to talk about what happened *after* one is dead. I shocked them all by remarking that if you *don't* know what happens after death, then you should keep quiet. If you do know what happens after death, then don't neglect to tell someone you know who is dying. Let them know what's coming.

Their reaction was the kind of quiet and seemingly pious scandal that can arise among highly educated people when faced with the Christian truths of salvation.

I look at death very practically. Anyone who is planning a trip loves to see a travel log with a description of what to expect. For heaven's sake, let's get out a folder on this thing and go over it with someone who is soon departing on that particular journey. The Lenten practices recommended by the church are extremely helpful in preparing for the voyage into eternity. Prayer, fasting, and examination of our consciences provide good chances to check out our spiritual luggage.

What have we packed for our journey? Some of us are over-packed, weighed down by excess baggage! We have worldly possessions far in excess of what we need, we have ambitions and desires for what may be damaging to our spiritual welfare, or we may have just plain vices. What can we just toss out?

What *haven't* we packed in our suitcases for our trip to heaven that we need to include? Have we packed a clear and unflinching commitment to the spiritual life—a determination to pursue the will of God at all costs? Have we included in our baggage a love for and sensitivity to the poor and those in need? If we took more concern now for preparations, we might significantly speed up our own passage through purgatory. Think about it.

Why shouldn't we tell those who are dying what we know about what's going to happen after they die? Speaking about the inevitable makes perfect sense to me. The reason we usually *don't* do this is because our society offers only platitudes about life after death. Many people talk about accepting death as a natural part of the human cycle—as if we were a bunch of cockroaches or vegetables! Or else we hear the "happy-hunting-ground" message about death, that everybody is going to the eternal cocktail party.

These common thoughts about death strike me as tragically vacuous. Christ did not die so that we could happily pass on into nothingness. And he certainly didn't die so that we could eternally imbibe heavenly martinis and exchange small talk. I agree with Peter Kreeft's observation: "The existential anxiety of the honest atheist confronting eternal nothingness is infinitely more noble than the vapid, bland platitudes of pop psychology about acceptance, coping, and getting your life in order."[2] These half-baked attitudes about death can easily creep into our thinking. Soon we forget the profound truths which the church teaches about our eternal destiny.

THE FINAL RINSE CYCLE: PURGATORY

I realize that many Protestants don't believe in purgatory. Every once in a while I run into Catholics who don't either, despite the fact that its existence is a defined dogma of the Catholic Church. For a Catholic not to accept the reality of purgatory is actually heresy. It is a beautiful doctrine, and when properly understood, is readily accepted.

Purgatory first of all means that this life is a gradual process of purification, of growth and change. We discussed our need for *lifelong conversion* in an earlier chapter, our need to break free from the clutches of unbelief, sin, and the influences of paganism. Purgatory after death is merely a logical extension of this process. Not only are we *eternally* saved by the grace of Christ, but we also grow in salvation and sanctification *while here on this earth.* As we learn obedience through suffering, we are renewed spiritually and become more and more open to the grace of God.

Neither the Gospels nor the letters of Paul teach that once we accept Christ, we sin no more. Some television evangelists who have made such a claim have soon fallen into the soup themselves. *If* we have not completed the process of purification during our lifetime, then God graciously allows us to complete it in purgatory.

Almost all world religions believe in at least a similar process, except that they may couch it in different terms such as *reincarnation.* The very thought of coming back to this wretched life again is quite beyond anything I want to endure. Not only do I not want to repeat a lifetime, like Frank Sheed, I do not want to come back for even one year. Yet that is what the Hindus, Buddhists, and many others think—that we get another shot at life. Forget it!

From the beginning, the church has taught that we have only one life to live. We are not in the middle of a dress rehearsal. As we each make our personal journey, we struggle to "put on" Christ as the Scriptures say. Paul exhorts us to "put to death" what is earthly, and to "put on" compassion, kindness, meekness, and patience (Col 3:12).

Many of us fail to finish putting on the new garments of Christ by the time we die. Even when we toss some of our old rags into the garbage, they seem to creep back into the laundry basket for another go around. The Catholic Church holds out the promise of purgatory to those believers who die while still at the laundromat of the heart. We will have a time—a *duration* if you will—to allow God to complete our cleansing before we take our place in the kingdom of God.

How many people honestly think that if they died today, they would go straight into eternal life and take their places forever at the banquet of the Lamb without any layovers? The majority of the human race falls far short of divine glory, even with the best efforts at scrubbing our stained garments and bathing in the grace of Christ. Thank God his grace and mercy extend beyond the grave.

In his vision of heaven, St. John takes note of the white garments of the redeemed:

> After this I looked, and behold, a great multitude which no man could number, from every nation, from all tribes and peoples and tongues, standing before the throne and before the Lamb, clothed in white robes, with palm branches in their hands, and crying out with a loud voice, "Salvation belongs to our God who sits upon the throne, and to the Lamb!"
>
> ...[The elder] said to me, "These are they who have come out of the great tribulation; they have washed their robes and made them white in the blood of the Lamb. Therefore are they before the throne of God, and serve him day and night within his temple; and he who sits upon the throne will shelter them with his presence. They shall hunger no more, neither thirst any more; the sun shall not strike them, nor any scorching heat. For the Lamb in the midst of the throne will be their shepherd, and he will guide them to springs of living water; and God will wipe away every tear from their eyes." Rv 7:9-10, 14-17

The Protestant reformers rejected the idea of purgatory because they believed it called into question whether we are saved by the grace of Christ alone or whether he needed our help—a spinoff of the faith-versus-works issue. Christ certainly does not need our help; he waits for our *cooperation*. That's a far different matter. He needs us to *accept* the purification he freely gives us.

Without a doubt, our robes are washed and made white in the blood of the Lamb. Because of his death and resurrection, we are cleansed from the stain of original sin. We are also freed from all other sin by his saving grace when we accept it. If grace makes us completely open to God and receptive to his will, why do the redeemed walk around looking so unredeemed most of the time?

To die in the state of grace, to die redeemed by Christ, does not mean that we are completely prepared to enter into the kingdom of God. After the moment of Baptism, very few people attain even a minute of complete holiness and sanctity in this life, even among those who try to be totally open and docile to God's will. I may go kicking and screaming into the grave. As the Irish saying goes, "Pride dies a half hour after you do." Yet God never gives up on us. He graciously gives us countless opportunities to put pride to death sooner.

Jesus promised the Holy Spirit would be with us to lead us into all truth, to convict us of sin, to help us to turn our hearts to God. During trials, how many of us listen perfectly? I don't know about you, but my ears often seem plugged with cotton. I'm glad I've been redeemed by Jesus Christ so that death is not the end of my journey.

If you don't believe in purgatory, you should never pray for the dead. They would already be in either heaven or hell. In the first case, they don't need your prayers; in the other, they can't use them. Yet I have met many Protestants who do pray for the dead. Perhaps this is no less logical than our own neglect as Catholics. If we took purgatory a little more seriously, we Catholics would pray for the dead a great deal more than we do, just as we pray for our friends on earth. I'm a great believer in praying for the dead. Who knows what struggles they're having on their journey—even though they are already at peace, knowing that they are saved?

Everybody assumes, of course, that purgatory lasts only a few weeks, months, or years at most. Why? How do we know that? Wouldn't it be disconcerting when we get off the boat in purgatory if our grandmothers are standing there to ask us why we stopped having Masses offered for them? Is it illogical to think that the next stage of our lives may be just as long as this one? Heed my suggestion: pray for the dead.

The reformers were also scandalized by the sale of indulgences for the souls in purgatory. Indeed, the practice was absolutely outrageous. Despite such clerical abuses, however, purgatory remains a beautiful and consoling doctrine. It has unfortunately received a lot of bad press, like huge pictures of pools of fire with naked souls bobbing up and down, with Carmelites and Franciscans pulling them out by scapulars and rosaries.

I would suggest that you think of purgatory more realistically. It is much, much better to realize that purgatory is not unlike where you are right now, although vastly intensified. *You are in a kind of purgatory.* That is the kind of place earth is. What did you think it was: Disneyworld or Epcot Center? As we all know, this life is a time of trial and suffering, a time of learning how to open our hearts to God. If the Messiah himself learned obedience by what he suffered, why should we expect to have any easier way (Heb 5:8)?

CARRYING THE CROSS

Jesus consoled his disciples in the beatitudes: "Blessed are the poor in spirit, for theirs is the kingdom of heaven. Blessed are those who mourn, for they shall be comforted.... Rejoice and be glad, for your reward is great in heaven" (Mt 5:3-12).

Neither pain nor suffering is good in itself. Both are the result of original sin. But so are psychologists, school teachers, priests, ministers, and rabbis. As a matter of fact, *most of us* would be out of a job if it weren't for original sin. I suppose in an unfallen world we might have still needed cooks, but maybe not even carpenters or tailors.

Once we accept pain and suffering, and the value they have in purifying us, we can go on in spite of them. Jesus tells each of us to pick up our crosses and carry them. When we do, our long-suffering becomes a powerful prayer, an act of worship. We have the examples of our Lord Jesus Christ, our Blessed Lady, and the saints who patiently endured the cross before us.

One of the crosses that may come to us is that of a painful death. Thanks to the great strides of modern medicine, many of us face such an eventuality. The terminally ill rarely leave in a few days anymore, but often take several months to do what our grandmothers and grandfathers could have done in an afternoon! So, what should we do? Don't worry about it! A painful death could be a marvelous opportunity to pray for others, to surrender our souls to God, to prepare for eternity, to purify our wills and open them to God's will.

Flannery O'Connor, the writer who suffered many years from lupus and other illnesses, said, "To die without suffering is to experience an unprovided death." If we should have such a provision, the Lord will give us the strength to face it. Don't fret about it now. What you think you may not be able to endure at this point in your life can certainly become possible with the help of God.

Having said all that, I am personally comforted by having been told by my cardiologist that I'm the type of person who is likely to die in my sleep. That could be difficult because I don't get much of it. But I'm always sure to say my night prayers very carefully. So what if I have disease of the arteries which is ultimately fatal? So is life.

Perhaps I'll manage to get hit by some carcinogenic substance somewhere along the way and end up facing a long and painful death after all. Living in the New York metropolitan area must surely put me in harm's way. I was thinking of leaving my funeral sermon on audiotape to deliver several parting shots, but came to the conclusion that would be a bit cheeky.

But I have a wonderful idea. If I do face the trial of prolonged suffering, I plan to put it on videocassette, with three or four little talks during the final stages of my illness. Maybe I'll entitle the set something like "It's Later than You Think" or "Greetings from the Other Side." If I make it to the last talk, the Daughters of St. Paul can put it out as a handy little gift package to bring to someone who is dying. They might appreciate someone speaking honestly to them about what is going to happen.

As a matter of fact, you might say a little prayer for me that I don't go too quickly, so that I can do such a series. A videotape on death would really be much more helpful for the dying than talking about the weather, the Mets, or the international situation. Since our culture has such a fear of death, we tend to talk about anything else. Somebody is sitting there dying and we're babbling on about what's going to happen next year. Face facts! That person won't be here next year.

You may think I'm joking, but in ages of greater faith, people talked about death quite openly. Even up to the time of St. Thérèse of Lisieux, people brought lists of deceased loved ones for the dying person to greet on the other side. I myself have done that. While talking to a dying friend, I think nothing of saying something like, "When you get on the other side, please say hello to my parents and Cardinal Cooke for me."

I said that to a monsignor recently who was dying. For five years I would ask, "How are you doing, Bobby?" "Great for someone who is dying of cancer," was his unfailing reply. When he finally was dying, I said, "Look, when you get on the other side, there are a few people I would like you to greet for me."

Don't be so macabre about death. It's coming. Many things in life are worse than death. Death can be a very gentle sleep, a sweet passing over to the other side. You close your eyes one last time and you open them in eternity. Why be worried? Why be afraid? Our human instinct is to back away, but our faith should help us face it head-on.

An eighty-year-old Spanish lady named Angelica came to visit us friars one morning and told us she was going to die at three o'clock that afternoon dancing to flamenco records in a neighbor's house. Of course, we didn't take her seriously. Guess what? She died that afternoon at three dancing to flamenco music in a neighbor's house. Not a bit flustered, she just wanted to go first class to the clapping of castanets.

THE HIGHWAY TO HEAVEN

When we are young, we live in a kind of infinite present. As we get older, our thoughts turn to the future. Those who face much suffering, difficulty, failure, and frustration often find great solace in keeping their eyes lifted up to the mountains of eternity.

How many people have you known who have passed from this life with the certitude of eternal life? I remember very well my last visit with Cardinal Cooke when he was lying, close to death, in his small bedroom in the cardinal's residence. I went to offer him some consolation, but he ended up showering it on me. He referred to his final illness as "this grace-filled time." He was already unable to stand and his hands were turning dark purple. We spoke of many things, especially of times people had attacked him publicly. He said quite simply, "It was my fault. I did not make myself understood."

This holy man embraced his impending death with peace, humor, and constant prayer. A marvelous ending to a holy life. But he had been well-prepared. The cardinal's Irish ancestors for the last fifteen hundred years had believed that Jesus Christ our Lord can lead us through the doors of death. His faith was built on a stout and sure foundation.

Brothers and sisters, you and I must think more often about our heavenly home. God never meant us to live with our eyes fixed toward the ground. How can we catch even a tiny glimpse of our glorious destiny in that posture? Once when I was giving a weekend retreat to a bunch of tough captains in the Merchant Marines, I told them, "You fellows live with the two best symbols of eternity: the sea and the sky."

But neither the sea nor the sky is actually infinite. Any mariner knows that no matter how expansive the sea seems, he will eventually reach land. We used to think of the sky as limitless, but no longer. Space scientists have now deployed the Hubble telescope which they say may see to the end of the sky. Someplace it does end.

Heaven has no ending at all. The beautiful hymn "Amazing Grace" expresses this truth poetically: "When we've been there ten thousand years, bright shining as the sun, we've no less days to sing God's praise than we we'd first begun." Or as St. Paul quotes Isaiah, "What no eye has seen, nor ear heard, nor the heart of man conceived, what God has prepared for those who love him" (1 Cor 2:9). We humans cannot conceive of what heaven actually is.

Pascal, himself a great believer, said that even those without faith would be wise to bet on heaven. Because it is an infinity, you can't lose. Even if there were only one chance in a million, you would be mathematically way ahead to bet on infinity.

St. Benedict said that the purpose of the monastic life was to prepare people to return to their heavenly homeland. For most of us, the word "home" and the loving images of our childhood are possibly our best clues as to what heaven will be like. We look forward to going home, returning as little children to the place of ultimate safety. I pity those poor souls who have suffered serious abuse early in life. Because of this terrible scar on their hearts, they usually feel they have no home. No image of heaven comes easily to them.

Those who try to make a heaven out of this earth often become embittered and find life unendurable. For example, consider the fact that the suicide rate in Sweden is a thousand times higher than the suicide rate in Haiti, one of the poorest countries in the world. Most Haitians cling to life, even in the midst of desperate poverty. Those I have met tend to be happy people.

I often pray that St. Brigit of Sweden would come back from the dead and see what she could do to brighten up her homeland. If I were given the choice of living there or in Haiti, it would take me all of a second to make up my mind. I would much rather suffer with the poor in Haiti than be tempted to suicide in the midst of plenty in Sweden.

I have spoken to devout Christians in Sweden who put up with its secularism, who try to keep the flame of faith alive amidst rampant depression. Then again, perhaps if I had more guts, I would want to live in Sweden rather than Haiti. How desperately Swedes need to hear the good news of Jesus Christ!

"You have made us for yourself, O God, and our hearts are restless until they find their rest in you." In our own meditations, we must often stop and think about where we are going. What is our destiny? Our destination? Those who want to be complete human beings must live with heaven in their sights; otherwise, they will lose track of who they are and where they are going.

The ultimate purpose of life is to go to heaven, an astounding prospect which none of us deserves. The full meaning of the wondrous gift of salvation which God offers to each one of us will be realized only in the glory of eternity. The final chapters of Revelation paint a vivid picture of this final homeland in the courts of our Father:

Then I saw a new heaven and a new earth; for the first heaven and the first earth had passed away, and the sea was no more. And I saw the holy city, new Jerusalem, coming down out of heaven from God, prepared as a bride adorned for her husband; and I heard a great voice from the throne saying, "Behold, the dwelling of God is with men. He will dwell with them, and they shall be his people, and God himself will be with them; he will wipe away every tear from their eyes, and death shall be no more, neither shall there be mourning nor crying nor pain any more, for the former things have passed away." **Rv 21: 1-4**

John goes on to describe a place of spectacular riches (Rv 22:1-5). Rather than smell the stench of sewage or breathe polluted air, we can drink deeply from the river of the water of life which flows from the throne of the Lamb. With no need to till the ground we have exhausted and denuded, we can reach up and pluck one of the twelve kinds of lush fruit growing on the tree of life. Rather than drag our sick bodies to the doctor's office, we can gather the healing leaves of the tree. Rather than crying out in emotional and spiritual agony, we can spend our days in worship and praise of the living God. Rather than hide in the darkness of sin, we can bask in the eternal light of Our Lord.

◆ ◆ ◆

Heavenly Father, your endless day is the light that beckons to human hearts tired of the fading twilight of this world. Even when we try to foolishly plunge ourselves into the matinée of life, the end of each day reminds us that we are moving along toward the final scene. And so often when life is difficult or almost impossible, we wish to pass on to a better world where each succeeding day does not spell the end of the one that preceded it, where our best efforts are not frustrated by our own sins and the hostile acts of others—even those whom we love.

Good Father, you have called us by sending your beloved Son from that world of peace and joy to this place of danger, toil, and death. You willed that he take up our burdens and endure our vulnerability even to death. We your prodigal children are confident in you—in your mercy astonishingly revealed by your Son, even after your justice and holiness had been revealed.

Bring us home, Father, after the contest of this life. Bring back the lost sheep and summon those who have struggled even haltingly along the way. Open before us the great vista of the Heavenly City so that at the end of our journey we may look up and see its light reflected in the sky ahead. Give some glimpse to the eyes of our souls of that reality which eye and ear and heart cannot contain, so that we may not fail along the way as we follow your beloved Son on the road he alone knows and he alone can open to us. Amen.

EIGHT

The Last Things

"Nation will rise against nation, and kingdom against kingdom; there will be great earthquakes, and in various places famines and pestilences; and there will be terrors and great signs from heaven." Lk 21:10-11

O NE OF THE MOST DEDICATED CHRISTIANS in the modern era was the humble French priest St. John Vianney, called the Curé of Ars. This extremely humble man with limited human abilities practically revitalized the faith of a whole generation of French people in the early part of the nineteenth century.

John Vianney scarcely made it through seminary because of his limited intellectual talents and was then assigned to a dying parish where few went to church. This simple man of faith did the only thing he knew would work: he started to pray. He prayed fervently, and the parish came back to life.

Gradually this priest's reputation for holiness spread throughout France. He was busy night and day, frequently attacked by spiritual and human enemies. A huge railroad station had to be built in the village of Ars to accommodate the thousands coming to hear him preach and to receive absolution from him. St. John Vianney led a penitential and humble life throughout his priestly years. He was so humble that he even signed a petition against himself, circulated by the clergy of the diocese who were put off by his popularity.

As St. John Vianney was approaching death, his physician told him he had only about half an hour to live. His reply: "I go before the Lord with empty hands."

What an incredible statement. This man had spent his life in fervent, prayerful service of the Lord. Yet he saw himself with empty hands and threw himself on God's mercy. John Vianney intuitively perceived something of the absolute purity and holiness of God. God is holy in the sense that he is different, other, transcendent, completely beyond anything that we know or can comprehend.

Aware of the absolute holiness of God, the saints have taken the last things—death, judgment, hell, and heaven—very seriously. While the saints are concerned to be unworthy to approach the holiness of God, most of us act very much like we are simply going to walk into the kingdom of heaven to the angels' singing. As we approach the end of this book, we have to turn our attention to a very serious question. Who are we in relationship to what we shall become?

BALANCING THE ACCOUNTS

A missionary priest from Africa once told me about burying a convert who had once been married and whose wife had become an evangelical preacher. When she showed up at the funeral, this priest asked her if she wanted to say a few words. The woman promptly got up and announced to everybody that her husband had gone to hell (a richly deserved destination, in her opinion) and that God was going to take vengeance on him. Then she walked out of the church.

The congregation was astonished by her pronouncement. Many were angry because this woman had not known much about her husband's conversion, or at least did not think highly of his becoming a Catholic. But I will say this for her: she took death and its mysteries seriously. And anybody who attended this man's funeral never forgot what happened that day.

We all need to think more seriously about the last things—namely death, judgment, heaven, and hell. Many people accuse me of being behind the times. That doesn't worry me much. I actually may be *ahead* of the times—something like a sign of what is yet to be, sort of like the Ghost of Christmas Yet-to-be. Now isn't that a cheerful thought?

A sense of justice is not strong in the human psyche, although any of us who grew up in a halfway decent home probably absorbed some idea of justice from our parents at a very early age. Whether we human beings are just or unjust can depend on our own inclinations at the moment. We usually know what justice is and can recognize injustice—unless we ourselves happen to be the perpetrators of it.

God's justice is not separate from himself. God *is* just. That is his very nature. What he has made in the world reflects his being. When you look at creation, you can perceive physical and chemical laws operating with certainty. For example, when you drop a certain weight from a certain height, it will always hit the ground with a certain impact. Science is built on this sort of predictability.

Not long ago, I read a scientific article on the first moment of creation. Matter, it said, was in a form very different from anything with which we are familiar. Even atoms did not yet exist. But a group of physicists have been able to determine that precisely the same physcial laws that operate now were in control at that first instant. One physicist observed that it was nice to know the world was made by a God who is consistent.

In the same consistent way, God has a justice of his own. He has his own way of making everything square off and balance out. The healing of the original wound will be total in every way. No lingering sore spots will remain to fester and cause a new outbreak of sin. How absolute God's justice is, we see in the life and death of our Lord Jesus Christ. His crucifixion for the sins of the world, the price he paid, is part of divine justice.

The world today holds out few true models of justice. Rarely is complete justice rendered because we don't have a clear concept of what that is. Criminals seem almost surprised when they are told that they must repay their debt to society. The price is not really owed to society anyway; it is owed to justice.

At the Last Judgment, we will see the ultimate justice of God being meted out. Don't take this lightly. Our Lord says that "the day of the Lord will come like a thief in the night" (1 Thes 5:2). We are warned not to be lulled by apparent peace and security, but to stay awake and sober.

Jesus described what the Last Judgment is going to be like. All the kingdoms and nations of the world will be gathered, and our Lord will come and divide them like a shepherd separates the sheep from the goats (Mt 25:32).

Jesus also states very clearly his requirement of charity to the poor and destitute in the parable of the Last Judgment. He will say to those on his right hand, "Come, O blessed of my Father, inherit the kingdom prepared for you from the foundation of the world; for I was hungry and you gave me food, I was thirsty and you gave me drink, I was a stranger and you welcomed me, I was naked and you clothed me, I was sick and you visited me, I was in prison and you came to me" (Mt 25:34-36).

I once heard an amusing story of a wealthy man who died and arrived at the pearly gates. St. Peter said, "Look at your record! You're a rich man, yet you haven't given a thing away in your whole life!" The man defended himself, "Wait a minute. When I was in the sixth grade, I gave ten cents to the missions."

St. Peter was not impressed. "Wait a minute, I have to talk to St. Michael." So St. Peter calls him over and says, "Hey, Mike, this guy says when he was in sixth grade, he gave ten cents to the missions. That's all. What shall we do?" St. Michael answers, "Give him his dime back and tell him to go to hell."

I'm glad we can laugh about it, but one day it's going to become very serious business. Have you noticed in the *New Yorker* that scarcely a month goes by when it doesn't run a cartoon about hell? They're humorous, of course, but why do we always make light of hell? It really isn't funny.

I'll go into more detail about hell later on in this chapter, but first I want to make it clear that we are judged because God is just. *God doesn't merely act justly; he is justice.* He can't be anything else. Consequently, justice must be served. The scales must be equaled. The Last Judgment is a reflection of God's character.

But I've got some news for you. I hope it's good news. There is no "Big Book." Right now, this very moment, you are the cumulative sum of all you have been. Consequently, nobody has to take time to count anything up at the time of your death. We *are* all the bottom line, each for our individual selves. We *are* everything we have ever been, everything we have ever said, everything we have ever done up until now.

We may not *know* the sum, but we *are*, right now or at the time of death, the sum. God himself will look at us with his piercing eyes of justice and discern our hearts in a split second. Don't think he'll need a divine calculator at the Last Judgment.

Almost all religions believe that God judges persons wherever he finds them at the end of their lives. This truth is so serious that Jesus deals with it in many of his parables and teachings. Be ready. Death comes like a thief in the night. If a householder knew at what time a thief was coming, he would be ready. If the servants knew at what time the master would return, they would be ready. We are told always to be ready for we do not know when the Lord will return. God calls us to get ready and to help others to get ready. May he give us grace in abundance to do so.

THE MERCY OF GOD

About two years ago, a man called for an appointment, explaining that he had been a priest in the sixties and wanted to talk to me. I set up a time and welcomed him to our retreat house. Not only had this man left the priesthood, but he had lived outside the church and religion for many years. Angrily, he had put it all behind him. Perhaps he had become convinced that he had been talked into being a priest, not simply by his parents, but by the culture in which he lived.

Suddenly, in a completely surprising way, the call of the spiritual life began to open in his soul, and he felt profound sorrow regarding how he had used his life and talents.

This ex-priest was almost overcome with grief as he sat in my office listing the number of confessions he had not heard, the sermons he had not preached, and especially, the Masses he had not offered. My heart was filled with a great deal of sorrow for him. I could see that he was in deep pain, yet I could say little that would take that pain away. However, I could speak about one thing that he would understand. It would not undo his past, but it could rebuild his future—that was, the mercy of God.

We spoke at length about how we all need the mercy of God. I explained to him the Catholic Church's renewed interest in God's mercy, especially because of revelations made to the Polish nun, Sister Faustina. I gave him a copy of the papal encyclical on divine mercy. This man has since been able to grow spiritually and to believe divine mercy is at work in his life.

Where would any of us be without the mercy of God? Believe me, although I have been a priest many years, preached countless sermons, heard even more confessions, and regularly offered Masses, I know that I am as much in need of the mercy of God as the ex-priest who came to see me.

The justice of God is as perfect as his nature, but this justice co-exists with mercy. God's love and compassion do not *undo* his justice, but rather balance it. God "picked up the tab," as it were, when Christ met the demands of justice by paying for our sins on the cross. Were it not for the mercy and sacrificial love of God, our fallen human race would have absolutely no hope of healing for the original wound.

Genesis tells about our fall from grace, and the rueful result of sin and pain and death. It also tells us of God's amazing promise of redemption, immediately after he has been slapped in the face, so to speak (Gn 3:15).

Just as we all fell through one man, Adam, so we are saved through one man, Jesus Christ. Perhaps the price of our salvation could have been paid in some easier way. Christ, the man, like all human beings, did not *want* to die. Jesus wanted to save the world by converting it. He tried many means, even miracles, to convert those whom he met, Jews and Gentiles alike.

The decision of the Son of God to come into the world required that he be *fully* human, subject to the full spectrum of human experience and suffering. Jesus did not have some fine-print proviso in a contract with the Father about not having to die if things didn't work out and people remained unconverted despite his best efforts.

Neither did Mary agree to become pregnant with the Christ child only with the understanding that she would someday be seated at Jesus' right hand as the Queen of Heaven. Mary's "yes" reflected her total surrender to the will of God, whatever the cost or outcome. She trusted God to provide the necessary grace.

Saying yes to the incarnation brought Jesus to the cross. The Father's love did not hold back his only begotten Son from paying the necessary price, even though it was an awful death.

The mercy of God is demonstrated most clearly in the crucifixion. No one could right the scale, no one could balance the accounts of justice except God himself. The Second Person in the Godhead, Jesus Christ, did this by coming into the world, and drinking the cup of the human condition to its bitter dregs. Ultimately it was not God but mortal humanity that made the price paid by Jesus necessary. A God who was merely just would have said "no." A God that was both just and merciful said "yes."

The mercy of God required that Christ take upon himself the weakness and misery of human life. How many times in the Bronx have I seen young children die unjustly, their sad lives snuffed out by drugs, violence, and poverty.

Miguel and his brother came to Children's Village after their mother had deserted them and left their father to cope as best he could. A devout man, he wanted the best for his children but was simply not able to replace their mother.

Miguel did well in our program and eventually returned home prepared to go to school. But one day, something snapped. Miguel, for reasons that I have never known, took a large dose of rat poison. Because of his youth, he survived and was eventually released from the hospital.

Then a few days later, Miguel stole a gun and ran down Forty-Second Street waving it. He was a tall boy and the specter of a seeming-adult waving a gun in the middle of the street set off panic on an already wild block. A plainclothes police officer shot and killed Miguel. He was terribly distressed to learn he had shot a mentally ill boy in his early teens. Miguel's father, a man of great faith, told the officer that he forgave him because he had only done the best he could.

As I stood next to Miguel's casket in the church of St. Rose, I was appalled, looking upon the corpse of a mere child who had been my altar boy, my choir boy, and who seemed to hold so much promise. But life on earth had always been just out of his reach.

I believe that young people so poor, so badly deceived will hear Christ say on their behalf, "Father, forgive them for they know not what they do." These little ones were born in earth's hell. They had precious little chance in life.

Jesus Christ died for Miguel. Such a conviction is not far-fetched, as we can see in the parable of the rich man and the poor man, Lazarus. As the rich man lies tormented in Hades, he calls out to Father Abraham for mercy. But Abraham answers, "Son, remember that you in your lifetime received your good things, and Lazarus in like manner evil things; but now he is comforted here, and you are in anguish. And besides all this, between us and you a great chasm has been fixed, in order that those who would pass from here to you may not be able, and none may cross from there to us" (Lk 16:25-26).

Unable to obtain even a cooling sip of water for himself, the rich man then begs that Lazarus be sent to his brothers to warn them, lest they also end up in this place of anguish. In a prophetic line, our Lord says, "If they do not hear Moses and the prophets, neither will they be convinced if some one should rise from the dead" (Lk 16:31). Jesus did rise from the dead and still most of his contemporaries did not listen!

It was divine mercy that foresaw the saving of the fallen world even in the first days of the human race. It is divine mercy that has repeatedly lifted the heavy burdens of this fallen world and made it possible for us to survive this long. It was divine mercy that brought the Son of God into the world where he demonstrated God's compassion. His death on the cross was the ultimate act of divine mercy.

You and I have a hope in eternal life *only* because of divine mercy. We must think about it every day. We need God's mercy and forgiveness every day of our lives. When we fail, when we show neglect, when we fall away, when we sin—perhaps several times a day—then we are reminded of our utter dependence on the mercy of God. Many people get caught up in raging with God, being furious at life, being angry at the church. If only they could experience and accept the mercy of God.

I once saw a bumper sticker on the flashy car of a young man which said, "Life is rotten—and after that, you die." I can only guess these few words were his attempt to verbalize profound disappointment, loneliness, emptiness, and lack of faith. They implied that people have no place to go after they die. Death simply means life is finished. Only then would the rottenness and futility be over.

Life on earth is far from merciful, inhabited as it is by many human beings lacking in compassion. If we all gave as much compassion and forgiveness as we ourselves want, the world would be a much different place. Nevertheless, divine mercy comes to us as a stream of living water filling our hearts with confidence and hope in a dark world.

THE FREEWAY TO HELL

The Judgment begins in this life. The highway to heaven is heavenly, but the freeway to hell is hellish. You can almost see the chains wrapping around a person. Just like Ebenezer Scrooge, people's chains grow longer and heavier the more tightly they cling to their worldly possessions.

I recently pleaded a particular cause before a man who is said to be worth three hundred million dollars. He was pleasant and seemed friendly and interested. To this man, my plea represented a small amount of money. A friend of his had told me this millionaire could forget to record the check and never miss it on the balance.

The man said he would think about making a contribution, but he never did. Yet he had said to me earnestly, "I can't stop making money. I don't need money; I don't want money; I can't possibly use the money I have. I'm old. I should have retired long ago, but I can't stop making money. I don't know what to do with it. I don't want to leave it to my family because they'll just squander it." Around that man's neck was an invisible, solid gold chain, like the chain of a slave.

What deadly poverty! What he neglected to say is that he can't even give his money away anymore. He used to be generous, but somehow money has gained a hold on him.

As our Lord says, "How difficult it is for the rich to enter the kingdom of heaven." If you are not rich, be grateful. You are missing one of life's great problems and one of its great crosses, as well as a very grave danger at the Last Judgment.

In contrast to the delights of heaven, the Book of Revelation paints another vivid picture: the destiny of those who have turned away from God. "But as for the cowardly, the faithless, the polluted, as for murderers, fornicators, sorcerers, idolaters, and all liars, their lot shall be in the lake that burns with fire and brimstone, which is the second death" (Rv 21:8).

Death is not an escape for those who will face this infinitely more dreadful "second death." Part of the judgment of God is the possibility of hell. The human mind balks at this horrible reality. I often found it difficult to think about it myself, until I visited the Nazi concentration camp at Dachau.

I had insisted to the priest, who had asked me to give the military chaplains a retreat, that I wanted to see this camp where several of my friends had suffered horribly. Dachau is now a deceptively peaceful looking historical sight. Three chapels—Protestant, Jewish, and Catholic—serve as stark reminders of the hellish things that went on there and of our need to pray that never again will such inhumanity be allowed to stain the earth.

Behind the chapels sits the Convent of the Holy Blood, inhabited by Carmelite nuns. This cloister of reparation is the home of German contemplative sisters whose presence hallows the diabolical Dachau grounds. The bell tower of the convent was once the gun tower of the camp. When one recalls what happened in this place and listens to the nuns chanting their psalms of praise, both hell and heaven seem near.

On the walls of the Dachau museum hang gruesome photographs of human beings tortured to death. Some even appear to be crucified; the weight of their lifeless bodies hang with their arms twisted behind them. These pictures were enough to convince me that hell is in the hearts of some human beings. But the clearest image of hell was not on the tortured faces of the prisoners, but on the complacent ones of those in charge of their torture, the SS guards. In photos, these men and women were sometimes laughing at their victims. One picture shows the guards sitting at a table with their German shepherd dog having a jovial beer party. The caption underneath was chilling: "And where are they now?"

Even more terrifying were the dispassionate faces of the medical doctors who used Dachau as a laboratory for gruesome experiments. One picture showed physicians freezing a man to death while calmly recording the results. In that most awful visage of hell, the original wound was like a bottomless inferno into which these doctors were falling, mindless of their ghastly demise.

If you examine the lives of many hardened criminals, you often discover that they have been badly abused. These beaten-down, twisted people do not represent hell for me so much as those who have become perverted in subtler ways. The doctors at Dachau had led privileged lives. They had been raised in respectable homes and received excellent educations.

Many of those who reject Christ do not bear the terrible scars from outright abuse, but nonetheless become willing to do evil by using other people for their own ends and purposes. C.S. Lewis' classic, *Screwtape Letters*, reveals the endless psychological weapons used by Satan to entice and capture human prey. He vividly describes debates and seminars on the eternal verities being pursued in the depths of hell.

Believing in hell may not be so hard, but what you may not realize is that hell is part of divine mercy. God does not make hell. God cannot make anything bad. *Hell is a place where those who have turned away from God forever hide from him.* Those who have spent their lives running from God are *least* miserable in hell, not most miserable.

St. Catherine of Siena tells a parable about going down into hell and pulling a lost soul up into heaven. The tormented soul rushes quickly before the throne of God. To offer thanks for being rescued? No! The soul cries out in anguish, "Will you get this crazy person out of my life? I was miserable enough in hell, but now she has brought me up here where I realize what I have lost and I am in infinite torture."

The French playwright Sartre wrote a play entitled *No Exit*. When I saw it performed, I was ready to run screaming into the street by the middle of the play. Three nasty, cruel strangers are in a hotel room, with a busboy running in and out, interminably, with anything they want. They finally exclaim, "We'd rather be in hell!" The busboy says, "Oh, didn't you know? This is hell."

When we seriously consider it, the eternal loss of one's true destiny is absolutely horrible. Even our Lord speaks of hell in terrifying ways. Medieval artists and writers such as Hieronymous Bosch and Dante have portrayed hell as a place of horrid grotesqueness and misshapenness, a gross perversion of God's original plan. Today we tend to focus on the psychological agony of hell—the pain of eternal loss. Both physical and psychological comparisons fall far short. Hell is forever and consequently cannot be conceived by the human mind. It has to be experienced.

Hell is the chosen hiding place of those who look into the loving eyes of God and say no. You cannot go to hell by accident, I assure you. But people can go to hell without realizing that they are making decisions to go there every day. This is no accident; they are merely kidding themselves. Such people may be suffering from a terminal case of denial.

THE END IS NEAR

Jesus spoke clearly about the most terrible day yet to come in history: the day when the Judgment will come, when the world as we know it will be destroyed. Our Lord ominously warns us of the tumult and upheaval to come, but then reassures us of his final victory: "And then they will see the Son of man coming in a cloud with power and great glory. Now when these things begin to take place, look up and raise your heads, because your redemption is drawing near" (Lk 21:27-28).

The end of the world is not far off for any of us. It will come to an end on the day of wrath, the Day of Judgment when the kingdoms of the earth will crumble and Christ will come to judge the world. We have no idea when this will happen, but we have no reason to doubt whether each of us will be present for this awesome event. Our Lord says that even the angels of God do not know when this day will be.

But the end of the world for each of us is coming sooner than we like to think. Perhaps the doctor unexpectedly delivers some "unpleasant news": your tests have come back "positive" (which means negative). You learn that you have only a few months to live, perhaps painful ones at that. You walk out of the doctor's office in kind of a daze. For you, the world as you know it is coming to an end, and no one around you seems to know.

A young couple walks by, hand in hand, oblivious that an apocalypse is happening right next to them. A little girl has the audacity to cry because she dropped her ice cream cone, when for you the sun, moon, and stars are falling out of the sky. A cabbie blows his horn at some driver that doesn't move fast enough, while you hear the trumpet of doom sounding.

Your friends pretend there is nothing wrong. They say, "You're going to be all right," which can translate, "Don't bother me with your troubles; I have enough of my own." Or they say, "Gee, it's lovely weather today," which translates that perhaps they do care but just don't know what to say and that's not why they came to visit you in the first place.

A lot of people don't even visit the dying because they just don't know what to say. We don't like having our own brief lives interrupted by someone else's sorrow. Some may stop by the funeral home for a brief visit on their way out to a pleasant evening at the theater. They feel sorry for the people there and mumble a few words to express their condolences. But the show must go on.

Just the other night I went to a wake and one of the relatives said, "Father, come with us. We're going out for pizza." That's life. Nothing is wrong with going out for pizza on the way home from a wake. But when *you* are the one who is dying, you say, "How can all these people keep going while I am going to stop?" For you, the world is coming to an end—perhaps in a few days, perhaps in a few fleeting years.

That is precisely the moment at which you must lift up your head. This is the very moment you have been waiting for all your life. You should have been looking forward to it. Life is nothing more than a frightened, furtive, neurotic race against death unless you turn around and look death squarely in the eye.

As a psychologist, I am convinced that much mental and emotional suffering is caused simply by the fear of death. People desperately cling to the trinkets of life because they are afraid they won't live enough. Power, money, pleasure, even the illusion of security, all give the impression of extending life. Our Lord warned us that worrying about the length of our days cannot extend them by a single minute (Lk 12:25).

Although frightened of life, most people are even more frightened of death. So many people are stuck between the proverbial rock and the hard place: afraid to live and afraid to die. The saints show us how to look death squarely in the eye. St. Francis said, "I praise you, O Lord, for our sister death." St. Augustine lamented the death of his friend, Nebridius, by saying that his good friend lived with God:

There he lives, for what other place is there for such a soul. There he lives in the place of which he asked me, an ignorant poor creature, so many questions. He no longer puts his bodily ear to my lips, but the lips of his spirit to your fountain, drinking his full of wisdom, all that his thirst requires, happy without end. Nor do I think that he is so intoxicated with the drink of that wisdom as to forget me, since you, O Lord, of whom he drinks, are ever mindful of us all.[1]

The astounding truth is that a Christian dies *in Christ*. That is the glory of our salvation. Every newborn believer has the firm hope of participating in our Lord's glorious resurrection. At the end of the world—by a power no more mysterious than life itself or electricity or light or matter or time—we shall come back to life again. In the twinkling of an eye, we shall be changed.

May we manifest this hope by what we do. May this hope sustain us in the dark moments of life. May our bitterness, grief, and sorrow be lightened by it. May our glorious hope be in the resurrection of our Lord Jesus Christ, who says to us, "Be patient, I am coming soon."

CHILDREN IN THE STREET

Next door to our friary in the South Bronx sits a dilapidated tenement occupied by some of the poorest people I have ever known. The vastness of New York City is simply beyond them; the violence and crime of the neighborhood is all they know. When our St. Francis Center is not open, the children play in the street. A few have parents dying of AIDS.

These little ones seem unaware that they are poor, that their lives are balanced on the edge of destitution. As I look down at their happy games on the steps of the friary, these children become symbols of the human race. All life is teetering between life and death, between time and eternity, between heaven and hell. We are all on a journey. Do we realize this before it is too late?

Left to our own resources, we have as little sense of our destiny as these children of the poor. We are just as insecure, just as helpless. We have busy careers that occupy our time and affluent homes with toys that amuse us, just as the city street intrigues these children. Along with them, we forget that all this passes away.

As the children play, St. Adalbert looks down from the steeple of the church high above the street. For almost one hundred years a statue of this bishop and martyr has presided over this ever-changing neighborhood. His stone figure makes me think of God silently watching over the passing drama of human life: joy and sorrow, happiness and disappointment, life and death, birth and murder. Ours is an exciting street, full of action.

But there is a great difference between the impassive gaze of stone eyes and those of God who may silently look on, but is nonetheless intimately involved in every human life. Not a sparrow falls to the earth without the Father's loving concern. God's reality is so far beyond this passing moment—his today encompassing all of our yesterdays and tomorrows—that we must believe without seeing that he is, as St. Augustine says, ever mindful of us all.

If God could shed tangible tears, our little neighborhood, our city—in fact, the whole world—would be flooded. God does not weep because he is at peace. But in compassion he has sent his Son to weep with us, and more than that, to heal and save that which was lost.

This is the mystery of faith and hope. God cares. Unseen, he mysteriously reaches out. He calls to us by his Son, his only Son, by his birth and life, his suffering and death, his resurrection and coming again. He encourages us in difficulty, strengthens us in sorrow, gives us courage in times of terror or despair.

I can't make sense out of much of life, even about the lot of the children who play in our street. I can't even make sense out of my own sorrows and failures, and so many have suffered so much more than I have. But of this I am sure, that death comes and with it the settling of all accounts. I know from faith strengthened by the deepest intuition that I am not destined for oblivion.

I must make my own accounting. I must decide each day if I will join with the divine law incarnate in Jesus Christ and his teaching. Or will I cast my lot with my own self-centered impulses which inevitably lead me away from all real love and justice, away from all joy of our Father's house, to the dark realm of those who hide their shame forever, as far away as they can flee from the love of God?

I am immensely grateful to know of the revelation of God to Israel, and of the revelation of God in Christ. I am filled with gratitude to belong to the Catholic Church, with all its failings. I am overwhelmed by the sacraments of Christ which touch the lives of those little children in the street and my own life with a pure, supernatural light. How grateful I am to be their priest and their brother! When these little ones call me "Father" or "Brother" (as people do because we friars make no distinctions of rank), I am delighted that I can be so called by the poorest of the poor.

In the face of the guilt many of us feel toward the very poor, I have been blessed to share their poverty, at least in some small way. God's grace, in fact, reaches out to all whom I love—my human family, my brothers and sisters in religious life, the poor whom I serve. I have only one great request of God: let us all be saved! Let as many as possible be saved! My loved ones and friends, my critics and enemies, the rich and the poor, strangers and all those so far away.

◆ ◆ ◆

Reach down, O Lord, and draw us to yourself. Restrain our evil impulses, open our hearts to good, to love, to forgiveness, to the fulfillment of your holy laws which call us to be like you.

Jesus, our Savior, knock with your wounded hand at the closed doors of our hearts and call to us in the streets of life. Give us direction in the confusion and cares of this painful journey. Stay with us, O Lord, for evening comes and the shadows grow long.

May your Holy Spirit fill the world with God's healing and strength beyond all our meriting or expectations so that we may be saved, and all those we love and the whole world. Amen.

The Great Healing

I FINISHED THIS BOOK at a beautiful and prayerful Benedictine Abbey in British Columbia while giving a few retreat conferences for members of the Society of St. Vincent de Paul, a group of dedicated lay people who work with the poor. Among the retreatants, I noticed a young man who was prematurely bald and showed signs of extensive brain surgery. In the early hours of the morning, he and I found ourselves at the coffee urn where providence provided the closing for this book of meditations on the truths of salvation.

Ed Born is bright and outgoing, full of life. He told me in those quiet moments that he had developed a malignant brain tumor ten years ago while a teenager. He was involved at that time with typical worldly pursuits, although he was a practicing Catholic. His friends quickly disappeared when he became so ill, he lost his job and, seemingly, his future. But Ed discovered a depth of faith that led him to establish a youth ministry based on Scripture and the Tradition of the Catholic Church. He put together a simple but compelling statement on—you guessed it— the truths of salvation for teenagers and young adults. This little but powerful booklet is entitled, paradoxically, *Understanding Life and Living It.*[1] I say "paradoxically" because a young person with a brain tumor has a physical life that is at least problematic.

Ed's cancer, in fact, recurred last year and he has been undergoing chemotherapy. But he is still full of life.

As we sat in the early dawn in the refectory, I felt great awe. Ed spoke so quietly, so unpretentiously, that I realized I was in the presence of both great suffering and great faith. There the truths of salvation came together in ways that are beyond expression, as they so often are. Suffering asks the great questions of life. In itself suffering is only a by-product of life as we know it, a consequence of our fragile existence and wounded nature. But it becomes the occasion for faith and hope, and even for love. We must ask the question "Why" when suffering occurs, but we must be prepared to listen to an answer which may be as mysterious as the question. The explanation of great suffering may be likened to the bright light of a distant sun breaking through dark clouds at the end of a storm. The answer sheds light, but it is dim compared to its source, which we have yet to reach. It ultimately remains shrouded in mystery.

Ed has no illusions. We spoke about the fact that he is dying, that I am dying, that we are all dying. He has the possibility of terminal illness to remind him forcefully of the mortality that we all share. But Ed is living far more fully than he might have, had he never developed cancer. He works energetically to bring the gospel to the young. He brings to them a life that is not his own but that of Christ. He tells them of the mystery of how we are healed by the wounds of Christ, as Isaiah said we would be five hundred years before Christ's death on our behalf. I, too, have tried in this book, as innumerable followers of Christ have tried, to put this mysterious truth into words. But I know that my words are inadequate for the job.

When suffering comes, as it must to any human life, we need to turn to the mystery of salvation, the mystery of the cross. We can, if we choose, keep questioning. But as Padre Pio, the Capuchin stigmatist, said, "The habit of asking *why* has ruined the world." Or we can kneel before the cross of Jesus.

Another friend of mine, John Downs, founder of Apostolatus Uniti, became a quadriplegic in an athletic accident at the age of fifteen. The realization that he had a mind imprisoned in a body that did not respond was, as one can dimly imagine, devastating for an active young man at the beginning of life.

Yet I watched John from his electric wheelchair supervise a complex, week-long meeting of a thousand people at the National Shrine in Washington. So enthusiastic were the prayers night and day, that I think the Lord himself needed a rest at the end of the week.

Writing in a family journal called *Nazareth*, John tells us how a wound such as his can bring healing:

> Suffering is not understood by asking why a good God would allow evil but rather by humbly accepting the fact that not only does a good and loving God permit suffering, but that it is through this GIFT of suffering that we can begin to live authentically human lives and that a fallen humanity can become ennobled and elevated. In particular, suffering can help us to attain humility and detachment from ourselves through knowledge and acceptance of our creaturehood; to become love, as God is love; to live a more spiritual/contemplative life in union with God, which is the life of Heaven for which we were created.
>
> One of the first things that an afflicted person can discover is his own creaturehood and total dependence on God; that he is not the master of his own destiny. Through pain, dependency, and mortification, he learns that he is a creature, not a god. Herein one develops the only sure foundation for a spiritual life, a life of union with God, and that is HUMILITY.[2]

The truths of salvation, like all revelation, must take root by God's grace in the soul and grow. They are ultimately a mystery that must be entered into and lived, not simply a set of theological truths to understand intellectually. The interested person without faith can only dimly appreciate them, just as he or she might be moved by a great masterpiece depicting the crucifixion or the resurrection. The superficial believer, distracted by the cares of life, may even give these truths nominal acceptance until suffering comes and the pathetic reality of the human situation becomes apparent. The believer who prayerfully tries to follow the way of discipleship, despite failures and constant falls, will find in these truths the way to life in its fullest, in success and failure, in joy and sorrow, in life and death. As St. Augustine writes in sermon 231:

The Christ preached by the Church is not Christ rich in earthly treasure or Christ crowned with gold but Christ crucified. When this Christ was first preached to the few who believed, he was mocked by multitudes. Nevertheless by the power of the cross, the blind saw, the lame walked, the lepers were cleansed so that all might come to know, that even among the powers of this world, there is nothing more powerful than the humility of God.[3]

Notes

ONE
The Original Wound

1. Kreeft, Peter, *Fundamentals of the Faith* (San Francisco, California: Ignatius Press, 1988), 55.
2. St. Augustine, *The City of God*, Book XXII, ed. Vernon J. Bourke, (New York: Doubleday Image, 1958), 519.
3. Lewis, C.S., *Surprised by Joy* (New York: Harcourt, Brace & Company, 1955), 115.
4. Kreeft, *Fundamentals of the Faith*, 55.
5. Julian of Norwich, *Daily Readings*, ed. Robert Llewelyn, (Springfield, Illinois: Templegate, 1980), 41-44.
6. Julian of Norwich, *Daily Readings*, 45.
7. Julian of Norwich, *Daily Readings*, 45.
8. *Confessions of St. Augustine*, translated by F.J. Sheed (New York: Sheed and Ward, 1943), Book III, 12, 43.
9. *Confessions*, Book IX, 13, 163.
10. *Confessions*, Book VIII, 12, 179.

TWO
Hope in the Midst of Hell: Our Justification

1. St. Bonaventure, *Classics of Western Spirituality*, trans. Evert Cousins, (New York, New York: Paulist Press, 1978), 62.
2. Kreeft, *Fundamentals of the Faith*, 236-237.
3. Kreeft, *Fundamentals of the Faith*, 281.
4. St. Bonaventure, *Classics of Western Spirituality*, 87-88.

THREE
Help My Unbelief

1. Kreeft, *Fundamentals of the Faith*, 59.
2. Kreeft, *Fundamentals of the Faith*, 59.
3. Schnackenburg, Rudolph, *The Moral Teaching of the New Testament*, (London, England: Burns & Oates, 1965), cf. 34-42. Also see Benedict Groeschel, *Reform of Renewal*, (San Francisco, California: Ignatius Press, 1990), 79-87 for a practical application of Schnackenburg's view.
4. I am personally so convinced of the importance of Pope John Paul's teaching, that I edited his talks on miracles. They are available from St. Paul Books, Boston, 1990, as *Wonders and Signs*.
5. Julian of Norwich, *Daily Readings*, 55.
6. Catherine of Siena, *Classics of Western Spirituality*, trans. Susanne Noffke, O.P., (New York, New York: Paulist Press, 1980), 49-50.
7. Thompson, Francis, *Poetic Works*, (London, England: Oxford University Press, 1969), 195.
8. Joseph Mary Plunkett, from *Liturgy of the Hours II*, (New York: Catholic Book Co., 1976), 2329, cf. Talbot Press, Dublin.
9. Fox, O.P., Matthew, *The Coming of the Cosmic Christ* (San Francisco: Harper and Row, 1988), 137-138.
10. Julian of Norwich, *Daily Readings*, 65.

FOUR
Conversion: Our Struggle against the World

1. Kreeft, *Fundamentals of the Faith*, 102.
2. Jung, Carl, *Psychology and Alchemy*, tran. R. Hull, (Princeton, New Jersey: Bollingen Foundation, Princeton University Press, 1968), cited in *The Choice Is Always Ours*, Philips, Howes and Nixon, ed., (San Francisco: Harper and Row, 1975), 181.
3. St. Augustine, Sermon 19, 2 and 3, as cited in the Fourteenth Sunday of Ordinary Time in the *Liturgy of the Hours*, (New York: Catholic Book Co., 1976).

FIVE
Sheep among the Wolves

1. Groeschel, C.F.R., Benedict, *A Still Small Voice* (San Francisco: Ignatius Press, 1993), 136.

2. As a Catholic priest, I have studied theology for many years. Despite the fact that Peter Kreeft is a convert to the Catholic Church—or perhaps because of it—I have found his exposition of these four marks of the church very insightful, as covered in chapters thirty-eight through forty-one in his book, *Fundamentals of the Faith.*

SIX
Growing in Holiness

1. Kreeft, *Fundamentals of the Faith*, 239-240.
2. Newman, Cardinal John Henry, *Meditations and Devotions*, (Wheathampstead, Hertfordshire, England: Anthony Clarke Books, 1964), 261.

SEVEN
The Door to Eternity

1. Kreeft, *Fundamentals of the Faith*, 155.
2. Kreeft, *Fundamentals of the Faith*, 155.

EIGHT
The Last Things

1. *Confessions of St. Augustine*, trans. by Frank J. Sheed, (New York: Sheed and Ward, 1943), Book IX, 3, 187.

EPILOGUE
The Great Healing

1. This booklet is available through the Society of St. Vincent de Paul, Catholic Center, 150 Robson St., Vancouver, British Columbia, V6B 2A7, Canada.
2. John Downs, "Into Your Hands" in *Nazareth, a Catholic Family Journal,* Lent 1992, Vol. 2, No. 2, 23.
3. St. Augustine, *Sermones Novi Testamenti*, Sermo CCXXXI, Translation is my own.